To Set Before A Queen

ROYAL RECIPES AND REMINISCENCES

BY

Mrs. Alma McKee

FORMERLY COOK TO
HER MAJESTY QUEEN ELIZABETH II
AND HER MAJESTY THE QUEEN MOTHER

Simon and Schuster · New York · 1964

ALL RIGHTS RESERVED
INCLUDING THE RIGHT OF REPRODUCTION
IN WHOLE OR IN PART IN ANY FORM
COPYRIGHT © 1963, 1964 BY ALMA MC KEE
PUBLISHED BY SIMON AND SCHUSTER, INC.
ROCKEFELLER CENTER, 630 FIFTH AVENUE
NEW YORK 20, N. Y.

First Printing

DESIGNED BY EVE METZ

LIBRARY OF CONGRESS CATALOG CARD NUMBER: 64-19936
MANUFACTURED IN THE UNITED STATES OF AMERICA
PRINTED BY MAHONY & ROESE, INC., NEW YORK
BOUND BY AMERICAN BOOK-STRATFORD PRESS, INC., NEW YORK

To Set Before A Queen

Contents

Introduction

How STRANGE it is to look back over forty years and realize that you have devoted most of your life to food.

Yet cooking is a large part of most women's lives. To some it is a chore and to others it brings pleasure. I enjoyed cooking when a child in Sweden because, on a simple level, I had found that here was a way to please people and make them happy.

I leave it to others to rhapsodize about the *art* of cooking. To me it is an expression of love and care. I think most women will know what I mean.

Male chefs in the great houses I have known produce masterpieces of *haute cuisine*. Magnificent in every way. If you do not happen to like a particular dish, then it is your bad taste—but that is not really the point. Is it or is it not a masterpiece? they query anxiously. Whether or not you actually like it is another matter.

This, I think, is the essential difference between the male and female approach to cooking. A man cooks with his head, a woman with her heart.

When I first went to cook for Princess Elizabeth at Clarence House in 1951, I was told that I was the only female chef in charge of a royal kitchen. I had previously cooked for King Peter of Yugoslavia and his wife, but that was different. They were very young at the time when I was there, and very informal. I had stayed with them until I suddenly developed pneumonia and had to leave in order to take a long convalescence.

When I got back to health my agency offered me a choice of two jobs. One was with Isaac Wolfson, the industrialist, the other at Clarence House.

I saw Mrs. Wolfson first. She offered me ten pounds a week and a promise of being well looked after when I retired. "If you come to us," she told me, "you'll never regret it."

When I went for my interview with the Comptroller of Clarence House, General Browning, I had more or less decided to take Mrs. Wolfson's offer, as I thought I did not feel equal to the responsibility of a royal household at that time.

But I had reckoned without the General's forceful charm.

He offered me six pounds a week and said, "You're just the person we've been looking for. When can you start?"

I said I would think it over and let him know.

"Think it over now and say yes," said the General, handsome husband of novelist Daphne du Maurier.

"All right," I said weakly, and I started the following Monday.

Like most Swedes, I was horribly shy, and on that first day at Clarence House I was extremely nervous. I knew deep down that I could manage the job and that hundreds, if not thousands, of people had enjoyed my food. But occasionally you might meet someone who does not happen to like your sort of food. There is nothing you can really do about it. Everybody has their own style of cooking. And at fifty-five it was too late to change mine. I prayed I wouldn't have to try.

With my first meal came the first royal compliment. It was to be the forerunner of many, for Her Majesty is one of the most appreciative people I have ever worked for, frequently sending messages of congratulation or thanking me personally after a special dinner. There is something quite riveting about her smile, and I can assure you that when that smile is leveled at you personally there is nothing you would not do for her.

Perhaps because Her Majesty is such a very inspiring person, I felt that my cooking was at its best during these carefree days at Clarence House. I had never opened a recipe book, and I cooked as always by taste, adjusting the flavour and adding to the dish as I went along. The ideas flowed, and I ceased to worry that perhaps in one day I would be cooking lunch for four queens, followed by a dinner party at which every guest was royal.

Despite all the trappings the real core of the household in which I now lived was a happy and united family. And I had been in England long enough to know that family life always includes dogs. The royal family were no exception; they take their dogs seriously.

Every day, when the Queen is at home, she personally feeds the corgis. A tray is sent up containing a jug of gravy, a bowl of meat and a bowl of dog biscuits. Her Majesty mixes and dispenses the contents and, when the dogs have finished, clears the things up and returns them to the tray.

When the Queen Mother and Princess Margaret were together at Clarence House, feeding time was even more of a ritual. Mother and daughter took rather a formal tea together at a small table covered with a white tablecloth in one corner of the drawing room. Then they laid another tablecloth on the floor, on which the dogs were given their meal.

The royal corgis fully appreciated their privileged position and had the full run of the house. At night their favourite sleeping place was under the bed in Prince Charles's nursery. By day they conducted a private war on the policemen always on duty to guard the house. The corgis hated their patrolling habits or uniforms or something, and in the kitchen we were always sheltering enormous policemen who were being pursued by these small but relentless dogs.

It would be naïve to imagine that royalty always dine off rare delicacies, though people are sometimes surprised when I go to the trouble of describing how to cook a good kipper or haddock, which the royal family certainly enjoy. Perhaps it is because the royal family, of all people, have no need to impress that everything is judged on merit alone. In my time at Clarence House, stuffed cabbage received as much appreciation as pheasant or grouse. More, in fact, as they were always overflowing with game from the estates at Balmoral and Sandringham.

When I first came over from Sweden between the wars and married a Scotsman, people were still eating seven-course meals in the grander houses. Now it is only on rare occasions that the royal family have five courses. Usually it is not more than three, and the food is good, but simple.

When the King died and Her Majesty eventually moved to Buckingham Palace, I stayed behind to cook for the Queen Mother and Princess Margaret. Before leaving, the Queen asked me to write down a selection of my recipes. As I was not accustomed to making notes of exact weights and measurements nor to describing my method of cooking in English (I still wrote in Swedish), the notes I wrote must have been decidedly sketchy. In fact, I felt sorry for the chef whose job it would be to decipher them. When Her Majesty reads this book, I would like to offer my profoundest apologies.

All my life people have asked me for recipes and I have suffered from the fact that my inability to reveal the details has been interpreted as professional secrecy.

For a time at Clarence House I was flattered to find that my name as a chef was getting known. By this I mean that it was known to the small circle of top-calibre chefs who are employed by the few remaining large private households, or who work for clubs and distinguished restaurants. These chefs, all men, invited me to dinner and in turn gave me their masterpieces, generously telling me the recipes. Or some of them. I asked them back and gave of my best. It was all very jolly until they asked me for my "secrets." Sooner than reveal that I had only the vaguest idea of how much of this or that I put into a dish, I had to preserve a mysterious silence.

This was the end of the dinner parties.

After this, and the inadequate recipes I was forced to give to the Queen, I started studying myself at work, as it were, and for the first time started weighing things and analyzing my methods.

The recipes in this book, though only a fraction of the dishes I have cooked in a lifetime, are some of the ones I have been asked for most often, and I am happy that I can at last supply them. I must, at this point, thank Miss Maureen Owen for all her help in preparing them for the press.

I am happy, too, for the opportunity of setting out a few of the true principles of Swedish cookery—a sadly unknown branch of gastronomy.

Swedes like their food. We like our food to be good and we like our food to be well cooked. Above all we like to be able to taste the *flavour* of that good meat, or fish, or whatever it is we are cooking. You will not find us flinging a glass of sherry or wine into a stew in the vague hope of making it more interesting. Instead our cookery is based on scientific principles more concerned with drawing out the flavour of the basic ingredient than obscuring it.

But perhaps the best advice I can give, for anyone who wants to make other people happy with their food, is to cook with love and trust your palate.

15

Taste the food as you go along and do not be afraid to adjust the flavour according to your palate. Due to temperature, season and type of storage, food is susceptible to a hundred and one variations.

As for love—no dish should be served without it.

Sauces

The English have over two dozen religions, but only one sauce, I was told when I first came to this country.

This is the most wonderful sauce for everyone and is served with fish, chicken, vegetables and with any meat that might be dull on its own.

The ingredients are:

5 tablespoons butter; 3½ tablespoons flour; 2 cups milk; ½ teaspoon salt; a pinch of grated nutmeg, pepper and sugar.

Melt 3 *tablespoons* butter in a saucepan, stir in the flour, add the milk and stir continuously over a low heat until thick and smooth. Add some more milk if necessary, then the seasoning, sugar and nutmeg. Let the sauce simmer gently for two minutes, then remove from heat and stir in the rest of the butter in small lumps until well mixed.

This is the White Sauce (or Béchamel Sauce), the basic king of sauces, which lends triumph and lustre to plain foods when smooth and creamy, but leads to depression and indigestion when greasy and lumpy. A simple sauce, a simple method, but greasy and lumpy it will most likely be if you do not remove that saucepan from the heat and add the remainder of the butter last of all.

I am a great admirer of the English White Sauce and use masses of it myself—but rarely, I admit, as an end in itself; instead I use it as the foolproof basis to a good many other sauces and dishes.

There is only one way to make a good sauce, and that is with love and care, which is why you cannot knock up a quick meal in a hurry and hope to put matters right by disguising indifferent food with a highly flavoured sauce.

Out of all the members of the royal family, the Queen Mother was perhaps the most appreciative of a good sauce, frequently sending messages of thanks and mentioning the sauce by name.

When I returned to Clarence House to cook for the Queen Mother after Princess Elizabeth became Queen and moved to Buckingham Palace, I was extremely nervous, since the Queen Mother had always been accustomed to a male chef. I was taken on under a temporary basis to see how we got along together. This was a point of view I perfectly understood, as in England all the really big kitchens are run by men and the administrative work of a large kitchen with a big staff is probably better done by a man. For although the Queen and her family numbered more than her mother and sister, the Queen Mother and Princess Margaret had a larger staff, most of whom had to be cooked for by me. Also, the Queen Mother and Princess Margaret frequently entertained separately, sometimes on the same day.

If the Queen Mother was doubtful, I was certainly extremely apprehensive, and at the last moment before she arrived at the newly decorated Clarence House I discovered that in the chaos of the move between the two households there were only two saucepans in the house. I had hardly met my new employer and my mind was blank of everything except where to find essential tools. The Coronation was imminent, and although the harassed Comptroller had not yet issued the program there was certain to be a huge amount of entertaining.

Into my mind came the soothing proportions of

❀ *Cumberland Sauce*

6 *tablespoons red*
  currant jelly
2 *tablespoons orange*
  marmalade (*the*
  thick kind)
juice of half a lemon
1 *wineglass* (2 *oz.*)
  sherry
pinch of cayenne
  pepper
¾ *teaspoon dry English*
  mustard mixed in
  water

Mix the ingredients together roughly and serve with cold ham, game, smoked veal, or hot or cold duck.

I do not remember with which meat I served this classic sauce, but it was a fortunate choice. The Queen Mother told me that she had not eaten this sauce since before the war and had almost despaired of finding it again. Cumberland Sauce is, of course, simple to make, but the proportions are all-important.

Rapport having been established with the Queen Mother, I went on to find other sauces that appealed to her.

Italian Sauce served with *pasta* is popular with all the royal family. And if there was a choice of several dishes to be selected by royalty for the following day's menu, this one usually won.

❀ *Italian Sauce*

1 *lb. chopped beef*
1 *large onion, chopped*
1 *glass red wine*
2 *tablespoons tomato
 paste*
1 *carrot*
1 *piece of celery*
2 *tablespoons butter*
2 *tablespoons oil*
*bouquet of parsley,
 thyme and bay leaf*
pepper and salt
2 *glasses water*
1¼ *cups grated
 Parmesan cheese*

Heat butter and oil in a heavy sauce-pan. Throw in beef and onion and brown. Add wine and allow the liquid to boil and reduce; then add the tomato paste, sliced carrot and celery, the herbs, pepper and salt and the water. Cover and simmer for about two hours. When cooked, add nearly all the grated Parmesan cheese and pour the sauce over *pasta*. Finish by sprinkling the remaining cheese over the top and serve very hot.

Boiled chicken and steamed fish are two things frequently fated to meet with White Sauce. Here are two sauces, white in appearance, but more interesting in flavour than the traditional Béchamel.

❀ Sauce Allemande

3 tablespoons butter
3 tablespoons flour
2 yolks of eggs
2 tablespoons cream
1½ teaspoons lemon
   juice
2½ cups chicken or
   fish stock
pinch of nutmeg
salt and pepper
pinch of sugar

Melt 2 tablespoons butter in pan and add the flour; stir for a few minutes without allowing it to brown. Dilute with stock and stir until it boils. Season with pepper, salt, sugar and nutmeg and simmer for ten minutes. Mix yolks of eggs, cream and remaining butter together in a separate bowl and add to hot sauce after taking it off the heat.

❀ Sauce Tarragon

½ lb. butter
2 tablespoons dry
   tarragon leaves
1 tablespoon tarragon
   vinegar
the juice of half a lemon
pinch each of salt,
   cayenne pepper,
   sugar

This is a cold sauce and requires no cooking.
Cream the butter in a bowl and gradually work in the vinegar and lemon juice. Stirring all the time, add the tarragon leaves, pepper and salt and small pinch of sugar. The texture should be light and creamy. Serve with all fish; particularly recommended for deep-fried Dover sole. For looks try warming two tablespoons in hot water and scooping out the chilled mixture so that it resembles a pile of heaped-up eggs in the sauceboat.

21

Mayonnaise is a lot more to me than just a coating for cold food. It can and should be varied in flavour to suit the dish with which it is served, and it also serves as a basis for many other sauces and dishes. Mayonnaise can be thickened for sandwiches and canapes and piped for decoration. Altogether a most versatile sauce, but one that cannot be hurried.

❁ *Mayonnaise*

4 *yolks of eggs*
2 *tablespoons vinegar*
3¾ *cups nut oil or olive oil (I prefer the former)*
¾ *teaspoon salt*
juice of half a lemon
dash of cayenne pepper
¾ *teaspoon dry mustard mixed with water*
pinch sugar
4 *tablespoons hot water*

Essential—a good whisk. I have a Swedish one made of birch branches which looks like a little brush. Mix egg yolks, salt and mustard into a paste. Then start dripping in the oil, whisking all the time and gradually absorbing the vinegar. Use the hot water, a little at a time, in order to thin the mixture. Continue like this, alternately softening and stiffening the mixture, for about twenty minutes. The lemon juice should alternate with the vinegar and hot water as a softening agent. Finish off by adding the seasoning and sugar and drop the last spoonful of hot water into the side of the bowl.

In all, the operation will have taken at least half an hour, but this recipe will give you a good quantity of mayonnaise, which can be used as a basis for a sauce or, thickened with chopped hard-boiled eggs, as a sandwich filling.

Some people go to extremes about the temperature of the room when making mayonnaise, but so long as you are not standing over a hot stove or operating in subzero conditions there is no need to worry. It is important, though, to see that all the ingredients are at the same temperature before you start.

All cooks need to have short cuts to resort to in times of crisis. My hectic days came about when the Queen Mother and Princess Margaret were living at Clarence House and frequently gave separate dinner parties with only an hour's interval between them. The food, of course, was always different. I don't think I ever used the same menu twice during the whole of my time at Clarence House. All the same, I often had reason to be grateful to my bottled mayonnaise.

The following are two entirely different sauces made on a basis of this useful mixture, and I used to look upon them as lifesavers.

❁ *Tartare Sauce*

1 *cup mayonnaise*
½ *cup whipped cream*
2 *tablespoons finely chopped onion*
half a dessert apple, cored, peeled and finely chopped
1 *tablespoon coarsely chopped capers, bottled in vinegar*
juice of half a lemon
½ *teaspoon English mustard mixed with a little water*
½ *teaspoon sugar*

Mix all the ingredients together in a bowl without cooking and serve with deep-fried fish or shellfish.

❈ *Lemon Sauce*

2 *cups mayonnaise*
1 *cup heavy cream*
juice of half a lemon
1 *teaspoon paste*
   mustard
pinch of sugar

Whip cream, stir in mayonnaise, gradually add mustard, sugar and lemon juice and serve cold with any fish that comes to mind.

This is another simple sauce which, according to the royal family, can't be improved upon. At any rate, they all ate masses of it.

❈ *Horseradish Sauce*

Make 1 cup of White Sauce, substituting beef stock for milk, and while hot add 2 tablespoons of grated horseradish. If fresh horseradish is not available, use double the quantity of bottled horseradish, but be careful to use a kind which is not too vinegary.

Serve with hot brisket of beef.

Hidden in among the sauces—a confession.

I frequently used garlic when cooking for royalty.

Apart from being told to curtsey whenever I saw Her Royal Highness and to avoid the use of garlic, nobody told me how to behave or what to cook when I first joined the present Queen and her husband at Clarence House in 1951.

This aversion for garlic, also shared by Princess Margaret, though not the other members of the royal family, seemed understandable enough for obvious reasons, and to start with I kept to instructions. One day, however, I "forgot." No complaints followed—in fact, there were compliments—and thereafter I continued to use traces of garlic in cooking undetected. In my opinion you never should be able to detect an overpowering flavour of garlic in any dish, and the cloves, if used whole, should always be removed before serving. The only time I ever saw a dish sent back with complaints from royalty was when an unfortunate chef once overdid the garlic and sent the result to table with the cloves still in it.

"We *never* eat garlic," came the message. Well . . .

The following was a favourite at Clarence House, and I can also remember serving it with Sunday lunch at Royal Lodge, Windsor:

⚘ *Pimiento and Tomato Sauce Provençal*

2 *tablespoons each of butter and olive or nut oil*
1 *pimiento, seeded and quartered*
½ *lb. tomatoes, skinned and quartered*
1 *clove garlic*

Heat butter and oil together in saucepan and drop in the clove of garlic. Add pimiento and tomato and simmer for twenty-five minutes. Put through sieve or mixer and serve with hot roast meat.

This is a sauce which is particularly good with all meat, fish or game which is inclined to be on the dry side:

❁ Sauce Rémoulade

4 *yolks of hard-boiled eggs*
3 *yolks of raw eggs*
4 *anchovies, chopped fine*
2 *tablespoons capers*
2 *tablespoons prepared mustard*
½ *cup olive oil*
2 *tablespoons tarragon vinegar*
1 *cup whipped cream*

Put the yolks of hard-boiled eggs through a sieve, stir in raw yolks and mix to a smooth paste. Add the oil and vinegar gradually while mixing, then the mustard, capers and anchovies. Lastly, stir in the whipped cream.

❁ Brown Butter Sauce

1½ *cups butter*
¾ *teaspoon black pepper*
1 *wineglass tarragon vinegar*

Brown the butter gently over a slow heat, taking care not to let it burn. Let the butter cool and put it through a fine sieve. Boil the vinegar and pepper in separate saucepan until reduced to half the quantity, and stir in the butter gradually. During the making of this sauce, the pan should stand over hot water and great care must be taken to see that the mixture does not boil. Serve with hot braised cutlets or fried fish.

⚘ *Tomato Sauce*

2 *tablespoons butter*
1 *chopped onion*
6 *sliced tomatoes*
2 *cloves*
1 *clove garlic*
light seasoning

Put all the ingredients in a saucepan. Bring gradually to the boil, lower heat and simmer for fifteen minutes. Strain and serve with lamb cutlets, steak, pasta, pork, etc.

The next sauce is a lifesaver. I first created it as a substitute for the wearying processes of Hollandaise Sauce. Many people mistake it for Hollandaise, and it has grown to be a favourite. When served with hot poached salmon, Dover sole or lemon sole or with cold asparagus, it makes a delicious dish.

⚘ *Sauce au Citron*

3 *yolks of eggs*
1 *cup light cream*
juice of half a lemon
¾ *teaspoon salt*
¾ *teaspoon sugar*
1 *wineglass of fish stock*
  if being used with
  fish, otherwise omit
4 *tablespoons butter*

Mix the cream, egg yolks and stock in a saucepan. Whisk until a custard-like consistency is reached, but do not allow to boil. When it is frothy add the slightly softened butter a little at a time. Finish by adding the lemon juice, salt and sugar.

Swedish Cooking

I would like to say something about the Swedes. Hardly anybody ever does. Honestly, now, apart from Dag Hammerskjold, some nice furniture and prohibition, how much do you hear about Sweden and the Swedes?

To their great disadvantage with the rest of the world, the Swedes are two things:

They are shy. And they are poor publicity men.

Their shyness earns them the reputation of being offhand and difficult. That song "Wonderful, Wonderful Copenhagen" got a lot of Swedes down, because although Stockholm is equally wonderful none of them would think of saying so, far less singing about it.

Sweden has many brilliant artists, scientists, designers and men of commerce, but somehow they lack the knack of telling other people about their achievements.

For instance, how many people talk about Swedish cooking in the same way as they talk about French, Italian, Chinese or Spanish cooking?

Yet there is such a thing as Swedish cooking, but instead of people knowing it for what it is—very good and distinctly savoury—various aspects of Swedish cookery have been gradually absorbed into modern cookery principles without anyone knowing where they came from.

Swedish cookery is scientifically based on health principles, but as well as that we like our dishes to be well flavoured. I have noticed recently that many recipes for meat and savoury food include a pinch of sugar. This is typically Swedish. For many generations Swedes have known the value of sugar in bringing out a savoury flavour. We also use other sweetening aids which are not apparent in the final result, like red currant jelly or treacle.

People talk about the salt of the earth, but for hundreds of years Swedes have known the value of its sugar too, and it is only just recently that other people have caught on as well.

I suppose you could say that my own cooking is a mixture of Swedish and English. I have a great admiration for good English cooking. I can think of nothing better than the British method of roasting meat; it is something that other nations admire and envy and seem incapable of imitating. I know this because frequently when abroad I have been called upon in desperation by hungry British expatriates to produce that simple favourite so difficult to the Continental mind, roast beef.

The British royal family prefer all that is best in English cooking as a staple diet, but have an open mind on food and like trying new dishes, always provided they are good of their kind.

As the royal family ate a lot of game, I often used Swedish cookery principles to provide variety. Although roast game is a luxury to most people it can become as boring as baked beans if served with constant repetition.

Despite all the grouse and pheasant on hand at Balmoral, Prince Philip's favourite dish was the humble wood pigeon. I remember him coming round to my kitchen window at Birkhall one morning and asking what there was for dinner. When I told him it was to be grouse, he at once went out with his gun and returned with a bag of pigeons, which I casseroled according to the following recipe.

❁ Swedish Pigeons

4 wood pigeons
2 tablespoons oil
2 tablespoons butter
1¼ cup stock
seasoning

Clean pigeons and dry thoroughly. Brown well with butter and oil in a heavy saucepan or cast-iron casserole. Add half the quantity of stock and season well. Cover and simmer for one and a half hours, adding the rest of the stock as required. When the pigeons are tender, cut in half and pull out as many bones as possible. Place the pigeons in another casserole and keep warm. Set aside the pan or casserole containing the gravy in which the birds have been cooked, and in another saucepan make a stock from the pigeon bones, simmering for about an hour. Strain off the stock from the bones.

For the sauce, you will need:
    4 tablespoons flour; 2 tablespoons red currant jelly; 4 tablespoons butter; seasoning; 1¼ cups cream.

Blend the flour with a little water and add to the gravy in which the pigeons were cooked. Add about one pint of stock from the bones and cook over a low heat for five minutes. Add the red currant jelly, two tablespoons of butter and seasoning. Remove from heat, stir in the cream, and pour over the pigeons.

Serve with plain boiled potatoes, peas and cranberry sauce.

This recipe is suitable for game of any kind.

❁ Braised Fillet of Beef

2 lbs. fillet of beef
¼ lb. larding bacon
2 tablespoons oil
⅓ cup light cream
2 tablespoons butter
1 wineglass sweet
    sherry
4 tablespoons flour
1¼ cups water or stock
1 parsnip
1 carrot
1 onion
2 sprigs parsley
3 anchovies
1 bay leaf
pepper and salt

Wrap the fillet in the larding bacon, tie with string and braise in a saucepan with the oil and butter, turning to brown all sides. Remove meat from pan. Chop the onion, carrot, parsnip and parsley and brown in the saucepan with the bay leaf. Season with pepper and salt and add the anchovies. Place the meat on top of the vegetables and anchovies and simmer gently for one hour. Take out meat, remove string and bacon, and keep meat warm in a low oven.

For the sauce: Strain the gravy and reduce it by boiling for ten minutes. Add the sherry and four tablespoons of flour and boil until the fat separates, then skim off the fat. Add the cream and, if necessary, more stock, stirring to make a smooth sauce. Strain; check seasoning.

Serve the meat with the sauce and accompanied by small boiled potatoes and carrots glazed with butter.

Prince Charles was a little boy of about four when I was at Clarence House, and Princess Anne a tiny porcelain-skinned baby. As I used to work in a clean white overall every day, Prince Charles called me the Lady in White—a nickname that subsequently caught on with the press.

I do not believe in nursery meals being dull, but often children get a craze on something and you have to keep repeating it until you can interest them in something else. With Prince Charles it was meat balls made from chicken or veal, though quite often in those days they were made from rabbit as well. At that time Prince Charles loved using the house telephone, much to the confusion of the office staff, and he would frequently call me in the kitchen and ask for meat balls.

Actually these meat balls are dignified under the name of *frikadeller* in Sweden, where they are a classic dish and are used in a variety of ways. *Frikadeller* floated on a dish of clear consommé, for instance, can be a smart dinner-party first course.

❀ *Frikadeller*

½ *lb. raw chicken*
½ *lb. raw veal*
6 *tablespoons bread crumbs*
3 *eggs*
1 *teaspoon salt*
1½ *teaspoons sugar*
½ *teaspoon pepper*
1½ *cups light cream*
juice of half a lemon
5 *cups chicken or veal stock*
2 *tablespoons flour*

Put meat through mincer three times. Soften bread crumbs with a little cream and add to meat. Stirring all the time, add some more cream and two eggs. Season with salt and pepper. Roll into balls or sausage shapes. Drop into stock and boil for fifteen minutes. The stock need not cover the *frikadeller*.

Just before serving, make the following sauce with the stock: Mix flour to a thin paste with water and add to the stock together with the rest of the cream, one yolk of egg, the lemon juice and the sugar.

Pour this sauce over the *frikadeller* and serve hot with mashed potatoes or rice and spinach.

In Sweden we also use *frikadeller* as an excellent addition to a cold buffet, or as a stuffing for chicken. And you can steam it as a *pâté*, decorate it with truffles and olives and set it in aspic.

Any housewife who has ever been caught with a last-minute party will have some idea of how I felt when one fine morning at Clarence House I was told that there was to be a party for forty-five royal guests that same evening. Added to that, there was nothing in the house, as we had expected royalty to be out that evening, and on looking round I found that we had no really big dishes.

The first thing I did was to borrow some enormous dishes from Buckingham Palace, rather like a young housewife borrowing from her mother in an emergency. The next problem was to think of something to put on them.

Everyone in the kitchen stared at me blankly.

"I'm sure you will manage beautifully Mrs. McKee," said the Comptroller serenely. "If it will help, I can arrange for you to have a car and chauffeur for any shopping you may need."

I jumped smartly into the car, directed the chauffeur toward Soho and put in some fast thinking on the way.

As usual I had to visualize the finished table in detail before I could start planning. As a matter of fact, I rather enjoy the stimulation of preparing a party. It is the dull everyday chores that clog the imagination.

On this occasion my centerpiece was:

❁ *Swedish Gammon (Boiled Ham)*

1 *whole gammon (cured ham) weighing about 8 lbs.*
1 *cup black treacle (molasses)*
5 *cups pineapple juice*
4 *cloves*
piece of cinnamon stick
ground cinnamon
Demerara (dark brown) sugar
dry mustard

Soak gammon for twenty-four hours if possible. Wash and place in a large saucepan three-quarters filled with cold water. Bring to the boil and remove scum. Add the black treacle, pineapple juice, cloves, and cinnamon stick. Boil for four hours. Allow to cool in its own juice and when cold pull off the skin. Rub dry mustard all over the fat and make a mixture of a tablespoon of ground cinnamon and Demerara sugar and spread on top. Place in a very hot oven to brown quickly. Remove when golden brown. Can be served hot or cold.

❀ *Braised Veal in the Swedish Manner*

2 *lbs. leg of veal*
4 *tablespoons butter*
1 *carrot*
1 *large onion*
2 *sprigs parsley*
1 *clove garlic*
1 *cup veal stock*
seasoning

Tie up the boned veal with string and brown in butter. Add the veal stock, sliced carrot and onion, parsley and garlic. Season well, cover and cook slowly for one and a half hours. When cooked, remove meat and untie the string. Remove the vegetables and reduce the gravy by boiling for ten minutes. Glaze the meat with a little of the gravy and keep hot.

Make the sauce from the following ingredients:

2 *tablespoons flour;* 2½ *cups milk;* 4 *tablespoons cream;* 2 *tablespoons red currant jelly.*

Mix the flour to a paste in the milk, add the remaining milk and stir into the boiling veal gravy. Boil for five minutes, strain into a small saucepan and add the red currant jelly. When this is well absorbed, remove the saucepan from the heat and stir in the cream. Serve meat and sauce separately.

An accompaniment of lettuce-and-cucumber salad with a vinegar dressing and small boiled potatoes braised in butter is recommended.

✿ *Duck with Prunes*

1 *duck*
2 *dessert apples*
1 *duck liver*
1 *glass claret*
2 *cloves*
1 *lb. prunes*
seasoning

Soak the prunes overnight in cold water. Core and quarter the apples and insert the cloves into them. Season the duck generously with salt and pepper, inside and out, and rub the breast with the liver. Stuff with the apples mixed with half a pound of prunes. Cover the breast with buttered greaseproof paper, place the bird in a hot oven and roast for an hour and twenty minutes, lowering the heat after the first half hour and basting the duck with its own juice. Remove the paper fifteen minutes before roasting time is up and let the duck brown without basting. While the duck is roasting, simmer the remaining half pound of prunes in water until soft, add a pinch of salt and keep simmering on a low heat. When the duck is roasted, remove it from the pan, place on a dish and keep warm. Skim the fat from the gravy.

To make the sauce, you will need:
2 *tablespoons flour;* 1 *cup stock (preferably beef)*; ½ *cup prune juice;* 1 *glass claret;* 1 *tablespoon orange marmalade.*
Add the flour to the skimmed gravy in the pan used for roast-

ing the duck. Add some stock and simmer for ten minutes. Strain into a small saucepan, add the prune juice, half a glass of claret and the marmalade. Check seasoning, strain sauce and keep hot. Serve separately from the duck.

To prepare a garnish: Pour a tablespoon of duck fat on the prunes, add the rest of the claret and simmer for a few minutes so that the prunes become glazed. Arrange them round the duck.

Excellent with red cabbage and new potatoes.

Perhaps after trying some of these Swedish recipes you will understand the principle behind Swedish cookery: the sweetening agents used in the recipes do not intrude on the final flavour, but serve to bring out the savoury aspect of the dish. Gravy is always reduced to preserve the essential juices and concentrate the flavour.

I hope you will enjoy Swedish cooking, and the next time you see sugar in a savoury recipe perhaps you will remember where the idea first came from!

Special Dishes

FROM MY DAYS at Clarence House a few dishes spring to mind that were special in a certain way. They are not necessarily grand dishes, though some are; others were made from very humble ingredients indeed, but I remember them chiefly for the pleasure they gave.

The following dish, for instance, I have cooked for more crowned and uncrowned heads than I can remember. On my leaving Lord Rothermere, his last words were a request for this recipe. The ingredients could hardly be more prosaic.

I will not strain my French, but merely call it plain

✿ *Stuffed Cabbage*

1 *large white cabbage*
1 *lb. of good sausages*
  (skinned)
1 *cup milk*
butter for frying
1 *cup seasoned stock*
1½ *cups beef gravy*

Cut out the stalk of the cabbage and parboil in salted water for five minutes. Remove, drain cabbage, separate the leaves and cut away the hard center and veins. The sausage meat should be taken from good-quality pork sausages, as sausage meat sold by the pound is seldom as satisfactory. Mix the sausage meat with milk to soften. Place a tablespoon of sausage meat on each cabbage leaf and fold round. If necessary, secure the leaves with thread. Fry the stuffed leaves in butter, basting all the time, until brown all over. Place the rolls in a flat-bottomed fireproof dish and keep warm. Then pour some stock into the frying pan in which the cabbage has been browned, stir and strain over the cabbage leaves. Add half a pint of thickened gravy and a knob of butter, cover the dish and simmer for twenty minutes. Dish up by boiling down the gravy a little and pouring over the cabbage.

Now that more turkeys are consumed in Britain, and at times other than just Christmas, people will perhaps be looking for new ways of preparing this admirable bird, so useful for serving large numbers of people.

There is a family feeling about roast turkey. It looks as good as it tastes; its very appearance speaks of good cheer.

I did the following recipe several times at Clarence House, both hot and cold. Although the preparation is somewhat of a fiddle, its satisfying appearance as the centerpiece of a party table, plus the delightful secret of its contents, makes the effort worth while.

❁ *Dindon Farci Rôti (Roast Stuffed Turkey)*

*a plump turkey
    weighing around
    12 lbs.*
FILLING:
    *1 lb. ground cured
        ham*
    *1 lb. ground veal or
        chicken (uncooked)*
1 cup cream
*4 tablespoons bread
    crumbs softened in a
    little warm milk*
seasoning

Clean the bird. Cut open from the backbone and carefully free the turkey of all bones except a small knob at the end of each leg. Leave the wings intact. Flatten the bird and stuff it with a mixture of the remaining ingredients. Carefully stretch back the skin and sew up the bird to resemble its original shape. Truss as usual, pushing the wings up and tying back the legs. Rub some oil well into the turkey so that it remains moist. Start in a hot oven, reduce the heat after half an hour and roast for a further two hours. Baste once or twice, but do not move the bird while cooking.

To serve cold: Baste with a little reduced gravy while cooling, to make a glaze. When it is cold right through, slice thinly right across the bird and put together again.

I take no credit for the next recipe. It was sent to me by a Government House in Africa where members of the royal family had enjoyed this speciality. Probably, because it comes from Africa, I always think of serving it on a warm summer's evening. I think, too, of a gold-and-white dining room in London, fragrant with flowers, and a young Princess not yet weighed down with the responsibilities of queenship, entertaining her friends.

❀ African Soufflé

8 *hard-boiled eggs*
1 *cup stiff mayonnaise*
2½ *cups warm aspic jelly*
4 *whites of eggs*
1½ *teaspoons gelatin*
1 *truffle*
1½ *teaspoons each of Harvey's, Worcestershire and anchovy sauces*
salt and pepper

Cut the truffle in half, slice one half for decoration and chop the other half finely. Slice two eggs and keep for decorating the top of the soufflé. Pass the other egg yolks through a sieve. Add the soaked gelatin to half of the warm aspic and cool slightly. Add seasoning, prepared sauces, sieved egg yolks and chopped truffle to the mayonnaise. Whip the whites of eggs and when they are firm add the reinforced aspic. Mix all together and pour into a prepared soufflé dish. Allow to set, then decorate with the sliced eggs and truffle and coat with the remaining aspic.

When I first went to Clarence House, Princess Elizabeth was the wife of a naval officer. Prince Philip's ship was in Malta at the time, and the Princess eagerly looked forward to their reunions. At times in that happy household it was just like being with any well-appointed, fairly well-to-do family. The routine ran smoothly, the domestic climate was calm. And there wasn't the same atmosphere among the staff which I learned to recognize later, of competition for royal favour when even a smile would be analyzed and talked about for days. So natural and informal was the atmosphere that often for weeks on end one would forget that this was a royal household watched by the eyes of the world.

True, whenever Prince Charles went out people waved to him and he would sometimes ask why. But the little boy took this to be a general manifestation of good will and waved back as part of the game.

But even in those early days, the Princess's private life was never entirely her own. Prince Philip had been on his ship for some time when the Princess planned a visit to Malta. Preparations were going happily ahead when suddenly one of the newspapers launched an attack on the Princess for enjoying herself abroad.

This criticism, unfair and absurd as it was, came as a bombshell to everyone at Clarence House and somehow cast a cloud over the preparations. The Princess went to Malta just the same, and as she departed the staff at Clarence House gave her a special send-off.

I heard that during his stay in Malta Prince Philip had developed a liking for *cannelloni* made in the local fashion, and I obtained the recipe. Somehow, however, I never cared to make the dish while at Clarence House. I have tried it since, though, and it is a good recipe.

✿ *Cannelloni*

PASTA:

7 cups sifted all-
purpose flour
4 eggs
1½ teaspoons salt
½ cup oil
2 cups warm water

Place the flour on the table, making a well, and break the eggs into the middle. Add the salt and oil. Add the water and mix without working the *pasta* too much. Cover with a serviette to prevent the *pasta* forming a crust, and leave for about half an hour. Then roll out fairly thin and cut rectangles approximately three inches by two and a half. Put into slightly salted water and cook from seven to eight minutes. Drain and put into a bowl of cold water, then take out and place on a damp cloth.

SAUCE:

2 lbs. beef or veal
lard for cooking
2 large chopped
onions
1 glass white wine
2 or 3 chopped
tomatoes
2 tablespoons flour
½ cup stock
salt, pepper, thyme,
bay leaf and
parsley
½ lb. finely chopped
mushrooms

Cut the meat in small pieces and fry, adding the chopped onions. Add the wine and leave to reduce. Add the tomatoes, then the flour moistened with a little stock. Add herbs and seasoning. Cook for forty-five minutes. Remove meat, put it through mincer and reserve it for the filling. Add the mushrooms to the sauce.

[*continued on page 44*]

FILLING:

1 *finely chopped onion*
1 *clove garlic*
½ *cup spinach purée*
2 *chopped lamb brains*
2 *egg yolks*
½ *cup grated Parmesan cheese*
stock for moistening

Fry the onion in a little butter, add the previously minced meat, the garlic, spinach purée, the brains and a little stock. Thicken with the egg yolks and some grated cheese.

Fill the *pasta* with this mixture. Lay the stuffed *pasta* in a buttered dish, sprinkle with cheese, pour on the sauce, sprinkle more cheese and add a few knobs of butter. Cook in a medium oven for ten minutes.

It gives me much pleasure to include the humble kipper among these special dishes. What is special about this dish is firstly the superiority of the best sort of kipper and secondly the trouble we take to cook this good fish properly. This is the *only* way to cook a kipper.

❀ Grilled Kippers

Real Scotch kippers, properly cured (not, horror of horrors, painted)
a kettle full of boiling water
one good tablespoonful of butter

Cut off the heads and tails of the kippers. Rinse them on an enamel plate in boiling water until they bend. Melt the butter in a plateful of boiling water and spoon some over the fish. Pop under a hot grill and baste with the butter and water. When you have done this once or twice more the kippers will be cooked. Perform the whole operation as fast as you can and enjoy the benefits of one of the few really special dishes that require the minimum of preparation.

Egg and Vegetable Dishes

AFTER SO MUCH rich food, it seems only fair to think about giving the stomach a rest.

Often, after cooking a fine banquet, I have enjoyed nothing so much as a light vegetable omelette. Just as it is good for you to enjoy your food, it is also bad to eat merely out of habit when you are tired or out of sorts. There must be many business-lunching husbands who would welcome a weekend of light but healthy food. There must be many wives, too, I imagine, who do not welcome a heavy midday meal. The danger is that the wrong sort of snack can lead to debility, overweight and other disorders.

My motto on food, if feeling out of sorts, is: *When in doubt, cut it out—but not altogether*. There are many valuable and delicious vegetable dishes which seem to be largely neglected in this country. Perhaps it is not thought quite proper to serve vegetables on their own.

On the subject of good health and sensible eating habits, I should like to quote Her Majesty the Queen.

For a member of the royal family, good health is indispensable. If you follow the Queen's progress in the newspapers you will find that she rarely has to cancel engagements for the minor but debilitating ailments that afflict most of us from time to time. Contrary to all the rumours I heard at the time, I have never known Her Majesty to go on a specific diet. Instead she eats from a varied diet which includes no fads or fancies but all the essential nutriments.

All that has been said about Her Majesty's wonderful complexion and sparkling eyes is entirely true. She is, in fact, one of the healthiest people I know. This is probably due to a splendid inherent constitution, plus plenty of fresh air and fresh foods. But there is one secret which may provide a clue to those glowing royal complexions—barley water.

All the royal family are addicted to barley water. The nursery consumed daily rations of it; it was always on the dining table. The Queen usually drank it in preference to wine. In fact, they all drank so much barley water that I felt there must be something in it and tried it myself.

When feeling at all out of sorts, a day or two on barley water is wonderfully purifying for the system; it is full of vitamins B and C, and, sure enough, it does wonders for your skin.

This is one of the few recipes I took with me from Clarence House, and in view of its beneficial effects I hope I shall be forgiven.

❀ Barley Water

½ cup pearl barley
2½ quarts boiling
    water
2 lemons
6 oranges
brown sugar to taste

Put barley in a large saucepan, add the boiling water and simmer over a low heat with the lid on for one hour. Squeeze the fruit and keep the juice. Strain the water from the barley into a bowl, adding the rinds of one lemon and three oranges. Add sugar. Allow to stand until cold. Strain off the rinds and add the orange and lemon juice. Keep in refrigerator.

Every family has its own favourite recipes. These dishes are valuable indeed, whether they be Mum's apple pie or Auntie Flo's fishcakes, for they are more than just a meal—they are part of the tradition of family life.

Buckingham Palace has its pancakes.

There isn't much tomato about them, but they are always called

❀ Crêpes d'Oeufs aux Tomates

2 cups sifted all-purpose flour
2½ cups milk
2 eggs
1 egg yolk
pinch of salt
nut oil for frying
Filling:
1½ cups Béchamel Sauce
3 hard-boiled eggs
1 cup grated Gruyère cheese
2 tablespoons tomato sauce
pinch of sugar

Place in a basin the flour, salt, two eggs and one yolk and mix well. Add the milk little by little, working the paste into the consistency of custard. Put enough nut oil in a small pan to coat the bottom and heat gently. When hot, pour the batter into the centre of the pan, one cup at a time. Work the mixture round to spread evenly and thinly over the pan. Adjust the heat to avoid burning. When batter has set, turn and cook the other side for one minute. Keep hot on a buttered baking sheet. Mix the Béchamel Sauce, chopped hard-boiled eggs, seasoning and sugar, and stuff the pancakes with the mixture. Spread the tomato sauce on top of the pancakes, sprinkle with cheese and brown under the grill.

Everyone has their favourite fruit. Mine is the Cheranties melon from Israel. Buy it on a beautiful day in June. It must be a Cheranties melon and it must come from Israel. Take no other.

Everything about the way you treat this melon must be perfect. So set a pretty table, if possible outdoors, and halve the melon with your best friend. Remove the pips with a silver spoon, chill and serve in your finest glass or china.

Eat and sit and think.

If your friend should feel that you have not worked hard enough, you could fill the melon with mashed bananas and sieved strawberries. It will be delicious but not as good as the plain melon.

French beans are terribly expensive and sometimes cost about 22 shillings a pound. Asparagus is cheap and vulgar by comparison. Make sure your friends know this when you serve what you laughingly call

❁ *Beans and Bacon*

1 lb. French beans,
   topped and tailed
½ lb. streaky bacon

Boil the beans for ten minutes or until tender in a covered pan of salted water. Remove carefully with a spoon and tie in bundles like asparagus. Place them in a warm buttered dish. While the beans are cooking, fry the bacon until golden brown; cut in strips and sprinkle on the beans.

❀ Celeriac (Knob Celery) in Cheese Sauce

1 *root of celeriac per person*
1¼ *cups Béchamel Sauce to two people*
small cup of grated cheese

Clean and peel the celeriac roots. Cut in half and boil in salted water until tender; then scoop out the centres. Add half the grated cheese to the Béchamel Sauce, pour the sauce over the celeriac and replace the centres. Sprinkle with remaining cheese and put in a hot oven for five minutes.

Everyone has a recipe for stuffed peppers. This is mine:

❀ Peppers with Risotto Filling

6 *green peppers*
½ *lb. chicken livers*
1½ *cups cooked rice*
1 *large onion, chopped*
¼ *lb. back bacon (Canadian bacon), chopped*
4 *tablespoons butter*
seasoning

Blanch the peppers by bringing them to the boil in salted water. Slice off the tops and remove the seeds. Make the filling by mixing together the rice (previously boiled in salted water) and the chopped bacon, onion and chicken livers fried gently together. Toss in the butter and fill the peppers with the mixture. Cover with greaseproof paper and cook in a medium oven for ten minutes, or until tender but not soft.

The following is a charming dish either as a first course or for a ladies' lunch.

🏵 *Asparagus Tips in Mousseline Sauce*

1 *tin asparagus tips*
  (*between two*)
6 *tablespoons water*
3 *egg yolks*
¼ *lb. cold butter*
1 *teaspoon salt*

Whisk the egg yolks one by one into the water and go on whisking until the whole thing is frothy. Bring to a heat just below boiling point. Whisk, lower the heat and whisk in the butter and salt until sauce is thickened. Pour over the heated asparagus tips and serve in a silver dish.

Together with barley water, there is really nothing more soothing for the stomach after a digestive upset than

🏵 *Oatmeal Porridge*

1 *cup pinhead* (*coarse*)
  oatmeal
2 *cups water*
pinch of salt
1 *teaspoon brown sugar*

Soak the oatmeal in water and bring to the boil. Add salt and sugar and continue boiling for an hour.
Serve with salt or sugar according to your side of the Border.

If someone you know is ill or miserable they might just prefer a bowl of very good soup. Not too ill or miserable to enjoy it, though, as this soup is frankly quite a lot of trouble.

❁ *Asparagus and Spinach Soup*

8-oz. tin asparagus tips
1 packet frozen spinach
1 cup good chicken or
   veal bone stock
1 tablespoon cornstarch
   mixed to a smooth
   cream with the
   asparagus juice
¾ teaspoon ground
   nutmeg
½ cup milk
½ cup cream
1 egg
2 tablespoons grated
   Parmesan or Gruyère
   cheese
2 tablespoons butter
seasoning

Cut the spinach into slices and halve the asparagus tips. Make a thick soup from the stock and the cornstarch mixed with asparagus juice. Remove the soup from the heat when adding the cornstarch and whisk well. Let the soup simmer over a low fire for ten minutes, add the spinach and let it simmer a further five minutes. Season with pepper and salt, add the sugar and nutmeg. In another saucepan, whisk the milk, cream and egg together and add the soup to this mixture over a very low heat. Still whisking, add the butter, the rest of the asparagus juice, the tips and lastly the grated cheese.

Do not boil, but serve the soup nice and hot.

This should do your friend a lot of good.

Once or twice a year, on a very hot day when there is someone special coming for tea, try this:

❀ *China Tea with Orange*

3 teaspoons China tea to
  2½ cups water
3 oranges
ice cubes
the juice of half a
  lemon
6 tablespoons brown
  sugar

Make the tea with boiling water and stand to draw. Slice one orange thinly and squeeze the juice from the other two. Add lemon juice and sugar. Strain the juice into the tea. Pour out and serve with floated slices of orange and some ice cubes.

Cakes, Puddings and Breads

DESPITE, or probably because of, increased urbanisation and the mass production of food, I have a strong feeling that the domestic arts are flourishing again.

I know a high-powered career woman in the heart of London who spends one evening a week baking her own bread. A glamorous model surprisingly produces a delicious home-baked sponge cake on a Sunday afternoon. The country woman scorns the instant cake mixtures and turns out a fragrant fruit cake made from a recipe that has been handed down from her grandmother.

There is a certain satisfaction contained in the smell of baking, the look of a well-risen cake, that nothing else can quite approach. It is a woman's way of saying that she cares for her family, and no shop-bought cake can say it for her.

Perhaps my happiest memories of Clarence House are of teatime in the nursery, in those carefree but numbered days when the Queen was Princess Elizabeth. She would spend the afternoon playing on the lawn with her two small children, carefully folding up the rug and taking in the toys when it was time for tea. Tea was always in the sun-filled nursery, informal and gay, with Prince Charles chatting excitedly about the day's events. Even illustrious visitors like foreign kings and queens failed to make it anything but family tea with everyone sharing in the banana sandwiches and sponge cake.

My most popular cake with the royal family was a rich chocolate cake made to my own recipe. Everyone seemed to like this cake, and it went everywhere. By special request I have sent it off to Windsor, Balmoral and Sandringham, and the Queen Mother asked for it for her birthday. Here it is:

❀ Chocolate Cake Made with Orange Marmalade

1 *cup butter*
1 *cup sugar*
2 *tablespoons orange marmalade*
2 *cups sifted all-purpose flour*
3 *teaspoons baking powder*
2 *oz. ground almonds*
5 *eggs, separated*
6 *oz. bitter-sweet chocolate*

Beat butter and sugar to light cream. Add egg yolks and marmalade. Stir in chocolate which has been melted over a low heat. Add flour, baking powder and almonds. Whip egg whites stiff and mix in lightly. Pour into greased cake tin and bake in a slow oven for one hour and fifteen minutes.

When cool, cut in half, fill and ice top with the following icing.

ICING:
½ *cup butter*
2 *cups confectioners' sugar*
4 *tablespoons coffee essence* (*instant coffee mixed with 4 tablespoons warm water will do*)

Cream all the ingredients together and warm slightly for spreading.

The cake looks nice decorated with pistachio nuts.

Everybody's main fear with a soufflé is that it may not "souffle," which is why, perhaps, there has been a decline in this delicious dish. The following is an easy soufflé; you can even open the oven and inspect progress if anxious, with no fatal results.

❃ Prune Soufflé

½ lb. dried prunes
¼ lb. dried apricots (if using tinned fruit, double the amounts)
5 whites of eggs
8 tablespoons sugar
¾ teaspoon vanilla essence
2½ cups water

Soak the fruit overnight, then simmer until soft. Strain the juice and pulp into a basin. Grease soufflé dish with butter. Whip up egg whites into a stiff froth and fold in four tablespoons sugar very gently. Then mix together the fruit and juice, the remaining sugar and the vanilla essence. Gently fold the egg whites into the mixture, pour into the soufflé dish and bake in a slow oven for half an hour.

Serve with cream or vanilla ice cream that has been dished up fifteen minutes beforehand so that it has become slightly softened.

Cooking for royalty is an honour, but it is no use pretending that the work in a royal household is not demanding. It would be easy if all one had to do was produce an inspired menu for royalty and bask in the glory of it all. But real life in royal households is not like that. In my time at Clarence House there were between eighty and a hundred *un*royal mouths to feed as well. Most lunchtimes there were about three different menus going at the same time.

First the nursery, whose menus were simple but needed careful preparation. Then the royal lunch, usually with guests. Next the staff, who ate substantially from a different menu. There were also the ever hungry policemen, who ate after the staff and enjoyed whatever was going.

Like any harassed housewife, I relied on some dishes which were quick and easy to make, but good of their kind. One of the most useful was

❁ Prince Charles's Summer Pudding

2½ cups fruit juice
  according to season
sugar to taste
6 tablespoons cornstarch
  mixed with water

Make the fruit juice with one pound of fresh fruit in two and a half cups water, add sugar, bring to the boil and simmer for five minutes. Strain. Boil fruit juice with cornstarch for three minutes and pour into glasses. Serve with cream.

Another nursery pudding which is also easy to do but sophisticated enough for the dining room on a warm summer's evening is this:

❁ Ice Cream with Black Currant Sauce

1 pint vanilla ice cream
1 pint black currant
  juice
3½ tablespoons
  cornstarch
sugar

Heat the black currant juice, add sugar to taste, thicken with two tablespoons cornstarch and boil for two to three minutes. Cool off and pour over the ice cream to serve.

Here is an apple meringue sponge cake with a difference. The difference, I think, lies mainly in the lightness of the sponge and the cream filling which flavours the cake if left to soak overnight.

❀ *Apple Meringue Sponge Cake*

4 *large eggs*
equal quantity in
   weight of sugar
   (approx. 1 *cup)*
half the weight of the
   eggs in plain flour
   (approx. ½ *cup)*
3 *teaspoons baking*
   powder
Filling:
½ *cup light cream*
¾ *teaspoon vanilla*
   essence
4 *cooking apples*
sugar to taste
Meringue:
3 *whites of eggs*
2 *tablespoons sugar*
1 *tablespoon grated*
   lemon rind

For the sponge cake, whip the whole eggs and sugar together for twenty-five minutes with a whisk or ten minutes with an electric beater. Sift the flour and baking powder together and mix with sugar and eggs. Put into a greased tin and bake in a hot oven for twenty minutes. Remove and turn out and when cold place in a flat fireproof dish. Mix cream with vanilla essence and spread over the cake.

Peel and core the apples and cook them with sugar to make a not too wet purée. Spread the purée on top of the cake.

Whip up the whites of eggs and fold in the sugar after beating, also the lemon rind. Pile it up on top of the apple and bake in a low oven for half an hour.

Keep overnight.

Home-baked bread is both impressive and delicious and not nearly so difficult to make as the amateur might suppose. And once you have made your own bread it is hard to return to the mostly mediocre shop-bought variety.

Try these two recipes one wet afternoon, and teatime, with the smell of these sweetly scented loaves, will brighten the day.

❀ Sweet Loaf

2 cups sifted brown
    flour
2 cups sifted white
    flour
2½ cups milk (can be
    sour)
⅓ cup corn syrup
2 oz. yeast
2 tablespoons chopped
    orange peel
1½ teaspoons caraway
    seeds
4 tablespoons lard
1½ teaspoons salt
white flour for
    sprinkling
½ cup water mixed
    with 1 teaspoon corn
    syrup

Warm milk to blood heat and add the brown flour. Stir well and work in the lard. Beat into a dough and add the yeast diluted in ¼ cup lukewarm water, also the syrup, salt, orange peel and caraway seeds. Stir into a stodgy dough with electric beater until the mixture is shiny and no longer sticking to the bowl. Sprinkle some flour over the mixture and let it rise in a warm place. Knead again if the dough is not stodgy enough and add a little more flour. Roll out on a floured table. Fill one-pound tins to the halfway mark and let it rise almost to the top. Brush over with the syrupy water and prick three times with skewer. Bake in a moderate oven and brush over again with the syrup water after half an hour. Bake for a further hour.

✿ Rye Tin Loaf

4 cups sifted rye flour
2 cups sifted white
   flour
1¼ cups yoghurt or
   sour milk
1½ teaspoons
   bicarbonate of soda
¾ teaspoon baking
   powder
1½ teaspoons salt
4 tablespoons melted
   margarine

Mix all together to a firm dough. Grease an oblong tin and place the mixture in a very slow oven for twenty minutes. Increase the heat slightly and bake for another 1½ hours.

This loaf can develop into a craze. Last time I baked it, I was asked for it again and again until a royal tour or holiday or something intervened. This was fortunate, as on the last occasion I baked it at Birkhall eighty people, including all the ladies in waiting, arrived for tea.

Here are some light buns suitable for nursery tea. I call them Chilean buns because I had the recipe from the Chilean Embassy after a member of the royal family had enjoyed them there for tea.

❀ *Chilean Buns*

⅔ cup sifted all-purpose flour
2 tablespoons butter
1½ teaspoons baking powder
¾ teaspoon salt
½ cup milk

Mix all the ingredients together into a hard dough and roll into a long sausage. Cut into small bun shapes, place on a greased baking sheet and cross them with the back of a knife. Place in a hot oven for five to ten minutes.

There is nothing nicer than pancakes if you have a hungry family to feed. I often used to make these pancakes after the royal family had been out shooting for the day at Balmoral.

❁ Sweet Pancakes

3 *eggs*
1 *cup sifted all-purpose*
   flour
1 *tablespoon sugar*
pinch of salt
1 *cup milk*
½ *cup cold water*
½ *cup cream*

Beat the eggs with the water. Sift the flour, sugar and salt and add to the beaten egg. Mix well to a smooth paste. Then add the milk and cream. Let stand for half an hour.

Cook the pancakes in butter until golden brown. The pancakes are very good filled with vanilla ice cream or with crushed strawberries or raspberries.

I have a low opinion of most mass-produced ice cream. At any rate, it has little to do with real cream. The following recipe will make you realize what you have been missing.

❁ Bombe Glacée

4 *yolks of eggs*
4 *tablespoons sugar*
vanilla essence to taste
1½ *cups heavy cream*
1 *cup milk*

Mix the egg yolks with the sugar in a saucepan. Scald the milk separately and add to the egg mixture gradually over a low heat, whisking all the time; do not let the mixture boil. Whisk until it thickens like a custard. Remove from heat and whisk until cold. Whisk cream and add to the mixture, pour into an ice tray or mold and put into the freezing compartment of the refrigerator until set.

61

❀ *Prune Pudding*

1 *lb. tinned or soaked prunes*
1 *oz. chopped almonds*
1 *lemon*
¼ *lb. butter*
4 *tablespoons flour*
1¼ *cups cream*
1¼ *cups sugar*
6 *eggs*
vanilla essence to taste

Mix egg yolks and sugar together for fifteen minutes. Add cream, flour and butter and whisk over heat until the mixture thickens. Remove saucepan from heat and continue whisking until the mixture cools. Add juice of lemon and grated rind and vanilla essence. Then add the beaten egg whites. Lay the prunes (stoned) and a little grated lemon rind on the bottom of a greased fireproof dish, pour mixture on top and bake in a moderate oven for one hour. Turn the pudding out onto a dish so that the prunes are uppermost. Serve with whipped cream and sprinkle the top with chopped almonds.

Can be eaten hot or cold.

If you like dark, stodgy Christmas cake, the next recipe is not for you. This is the cake that the royal family enjoyed. I would bake this cake on the 13th of November, when all the royal puddings were prepared, keep it and send it off to Sandringham for Christmas Day. This cake is lighter in appearance and texture than the traditional kind, but will keep equally well for a year or more.

❀ McKee's Christmas Cake

2 *cups butter*
6 *cups sifted all-purpose*
flour
2 *cups sugar*
1 *lb. currants*
1 *lb. sultana raisins*
4 *tablespoons orange*
marmalade or ½ lb.
candied peel
10 *eggs*
2 *tablespoons black*
treacle (molasses)
¾ *teaspoon nutmeg*
4 *tablespoons rum*
1½ *teaspoons vanilla*
essence

Stir the butter and sugar together until creamy. Add the marmalade and treacle. Drop in the egg yolks one at a time and two tablespoons of flour to each yolk. Add the nutmeg, then the washed and well-dried fruit. Mix in all the flour; add the rum and vanilla. Beat the egg whites well and fold in. Line a tin with buttered paper and bake at 350° F. for two and a half hours. Reduce heat to 300° F. and bake three hours longer.

Every year when I make my Christmas cakes and puddings I remember Christmas time at Clarence House. Some houses have a Christmasy feeling. Clarence House was one of them. This was probably largely due to the royal family; although they always went to Sandringham for Christmas, they created a festive atmosphere beforehand. Each year there were presents for everyone and each one was different. My first one was a very pretty inlaid trinket box given me personally by the Queen, who was then Princess Elizabeth.

Then just before the departure for Sandringham there is the staff party. My first party at Clarence House showed me something of the discipline royalty must impose on themselves even

63

at home. At these parties, the Queen would come round, chatting quite naturally with everyone in turn, telling them of the things she had been doing and asking about their plans for Christmas, and so on. Unfortunately I have no memory for details, but the conversation would go something like this:

Queen: "Did you know that So and So's [a famous catering firm] use —— pounds of smoked salmon a week?"

Me: "No, really?"

Queen: "Yes, I was amazed."

One was encouraged to chat back, and it all seemed very homey and informal; but I have noticed that, almost as if the Queen had a stop watch, she spends almost exactly the same amount of time with each person before moving on. In those early days, Prince Philip was more inclined to get immersed in conversation with one particular person or group. Polite conversation is not so much for Prince Philip; he likes to thrash a subject out and will cross-question you until he gets the full story. When this goes on for too long, the Queen has been known to give her husband a discreet sign to move on.

I felt sorry for the Queen over this, as, on the face of it, Prince Philip's behavior seems more natural and human. On the other hand, I knew full well from my experience in the royal household that if the Queen had spent twenty minutes with one person, leaving only a couple of minutes each for the rest of us, there would have been some jealous comparisons later. The same restraints are practised by the Queen wherever she goes, though like any other human being she must find some people more congenial than others. Unfortunately for royalty, if their patronage is not scrupulously divided it seems to arouse savage feelings in the human breast.

Fish Dishes

IF I HAD TO EXIST on one particular food in preference to all others, I know I would choose fish. Fish is nutritious, inexpensive and versatile, yet the majority of families eat it only once a week.

The royal family have fish every day, mostly in the evening, when a fish course is always included in the dinner. The fish for the royal residences is delivered fresh from Billingsgate every morning, as, together with staff and members of the household, we constituted a wholesale order. Milk, cream and vegetables came from the farm at Windsor, game from Balmoral, and meat from a small butcher in Staines. Groceries came from that well-known store in Piccadilly, and I also made regular trips into Soho for the sort of things you can only find in that district. I had a free hand with the housekeeping, though I had to make out the accounts in a double-entry ledger every week.

In the days when I was at Clarence House, strict rationing was still in force and although we were supplemented by game and poultry from the royal estates we had problems just like everyone else. For instance, the staff did not much like game. Then there were the royal guests, several times a week, who did not, unfortunately, bring their ration books with them.

I had great recourse to fish, and luckily the royal family were fond of it.

The following is a distinctly inaustere dish, suitable for about six people on some rather special occasion.

❁ *Fillet of Dover Sole Regina*

2 *Dover sole, weighing about* 1¾ *lbs. each*
2 *cooked lobsters, about* 1½ *lbs. each*
½ *bottle champagne or dry white wine*
1 *lb. lemon sole fillets*
3 *eggs*
¾ *cup butter*
1½ *cups cream*
seasoning and a pinch of sugar
4 *tablespoons flour*

Skin and fillet the Dover sole. Cover the bones and heads with half the wine and some water, bring to the boil and simmer for half an hour. Make a forcemeat from the lemon sole and six tablespoons of butter, passing it through the mincer three times. In another bowl mix the cream, 2 tablespoons of flour, the yolks of the three eggs and seasoning, and stir into the forcemeat. Dissect the lobsters and add any small bits and pieces of lobster to the mixture. Rinse and dry the filleted Dover sole and season well. Keeping the underside on the inside, roll and stuff the fillets with the forcemeat. Place in a buttered fireproof dish with the rest of the wine and cover with grease-proof paper. Poach in a hot oven for twenty minutes.

Remove the fillets and drain. Reduce the liquid by simmering. Make a sauce with two tablespoons of flour, two tablespoons of butter and about a pint of fish stock; cook until it thickens. Reduce heat and while simmering add the reduced liquid from the fillets. Remove from heat, strain the sauce and stir in four tablespoons of cold butter. Place the cut-up lobster on top of the fillets and coat with the sauce. Garnish round the dish with the meat from the lobster claws and some parsley.

Serve with button mushrooms steamed in butter, and new potatoes.

The following is a dish of the utmost simplicity, but one which repays careful attention to detail. The boning of the fish is easily done if a nice, clean slit is made in the stomach, and the backbone removed from the tail end.

❀ Truiton Bleu Royale

6 *blue trout weighing*
  6 *oz. each*
½ *lb. butter*
¼ *cup flour*
salt and pepper
Tarragon Sauce

The flesh of the blue trout should be a firm whitish pink. Remove scales, fins, and backbone, but not the head. Remove as many small bones as possible. Rinse well and drain on a towel for ten minutes. Open and season, then close. Melt butter in frying pan. Dip the trout in flour and cook gently in the butter until golden brown, about five minutes each side. When cooked place in a dish with a little butter.

Serve with Tarragon Sauce, cucumber salad dressed with tarragon vinegar, and creamed potatoes.

One of the pleasantest interludes during my time with British royalty was a stay at Balmoral while the Queen Mother was there with Prince Charles and Princess Anne. This was virtually in the nature of a holiday for me, as the Buckingham Palace staff were there, and such is the belowstairs protocol that I would not have dared bake so much as a cake without a formal request from the chef.

Toward the end of July there is a great upheaval in royal households. Preparations for the annual holiday at Balmoral start a week or so beforehand. Pots, pans, china and utensils—everything, in fact, except the Buckingham Palace stove—are packed up and sent ahead. On the appointed day the staffs of Buckingham Palace and Clarence House meet in the station at King's Cross and wait for a special train that takes them to Ballater.

On my first journey I remember being amazed that even Buckingham Palace could hold so many people, until I realized that many were taking their wives, families and domestic animals as well. The scene reminded me of some king from ancient history moving camp.

Whenever the Queen goes to Balmoral, Windsor or Sandringham the chief chef, Mr. Aubrey, his four principal assistants and a staff that varies from two hundred to fifty, according to the length of the stay, go with her. The remaining staff at Buckingham Palace then go on a system known as board wages. Board wages is an old-fashioned system whereby the staff can either eat in the palace or take the money to buy their own food. At the palace there are six male chefs and a staff of about five hundred, all of whom have to be fed. It would be impossible to keep all the royal palaces fully staffed, so every now and again there is this great move.

People often ask me how the Queen and her family manage to pass the time during all those summer weeks up at Balmoral.

The Scottish holiday is not dull. The Queen has a constant turnover of house guests. There are film shows almost every night, and several dances are given.

Out of all the palaces, castles and lodges owned by the royal family, Birkhall, the private house on the Balmoral estate in Scotland, seems to be the favourite. The charm of Birkhall is difficult to describe. It certainly is not beautiful, and it is far from luxurious. Princess Alexandra chose it for part of her honeymoon and the Queen Mother prefers it to Balmoral Castle. It is certainly warmer. Anyway, the royal family clearly feel that they can relax there, perhaps because it is such a contrast to the castle, where even to this day the royal family file from room to room in strict order of precedence—the Queen always walking first, followed by Prince Philip and the Queen Mother, then Princess Margaret, and so forth.

There is none of this at Birkhall. At teatime, when the shooting was over, everyone used to crowd into the not overlarge drawing room at Birkhall, kick off their muddy shoes and ask eagerly what there was for tea. The late King seemed to particularly enjoy these tea parties. He was not at all shy and reserved, as people often seemed to imagine. Instead he had a great fund of funny stories which he told with roars of laughter, and he liked hearing others in exchange. He would also take a great delight in a friendly teasing of his daughters and would go on until threatened with cushions and other forms of annihilation. These tea parties were, in fact, uproarious, and one had to fight one's way in with replenishments of tea. Then they would all go back to the castle with its rather curious traditions of formality.

At Birkhall the holiday spirit was everywhere, not least in the servants' hall. There was a piano there which was played until all hours at night, with plenty of singing and dancing too. Once at Birkhall, the normally quiet and discreet staff from Clarence House really let their hair down. There was no doubt that the noise percolated through to the royal quarters. There were no complaints, Prince Philip merely remarking to the steward in charge of staff that he was jolly glad he didn't have to control them.

As a matter of fact, there were several reasons why the staff should enjoy themselves in Scotland. There was a private golf course at their disposal, and tennis courts. There were also frequent dances for the staff with a private band, and a canteen. Then there were the film shows, to which everyone was invited. Sometimes the laughter and applause from the staff drowned the sound track, and the housekeeper, fearing that things were getting out of hand, subsequently apologized for the noise to the Queen Mother, who was then on the throne.

"Not a bit of it," said the Queen. "I like to know that everyone is happy and enjoying themselves."

The succession of well-known and distinguished visitors was another source of interest at Balmoral. It was rather like staying at a grand hotel where all the visitors are famous.

The Queen's favourite visitor, it seemed to me, was undoubtedly Sir Winston Churchill. The Queen was always frightened that he might catch a chill at Balmoral—a very real fear, as even in high summer cruel draughts would sneak round the vast rooms of the castle. So at the evening film shows she would see that Sir Winston's chair was not in a draught and, just to make sure, would tuck a rug round his knees.

For us the highlight of the Scottish summer holiday was the Ghillies' Ball held in September. Everyone, from the lowliest kitchen maid, is invited, and for at least a week beforehand all is preparation and speculation.

The scene as I entered the castle ballroom was an historic one.

Bagpipers in traditional dress played Scottish dances from the minstrels' gallery. The royal family in their beautiful embroidered dresses and tiaras sparkled like jewels against velvet in one corner of the dark-paneled room. On the night of the Ghillies' Ball, the royal family and their guests dance only with the staff. Everyone is issued with dance programmes and the royal family book up their partners in advance, sending the messages by royal pipers. It is a joy to watch some of the intricate Scottish dances, at which everyone, including the Queen and Princess Margaret, seems to be expert.

Everyone, that is, except me. Such steps are quite beyond me, and I fervently prayed that I would not receive a royal command. Fortunately, the royal family appear to know the limitations of their staff, and I was not called upon to take the floor until the Scottish pipers had filed out with a last flourish of the bagpipes, to be replaced by a modern dance band.

At Balmoral all the royal family lead an outdoor life, but of the ladies it is the Queen Mother who is the most energetic. Her great passion is for salmon fishing, and this she does with great concentration for hours on end. There is certainly nothing dilettante about the Queen Mother's fishing. She puts on waders and old clothes and is out to catch the biggest salmon she can find. She likes no interruption and takes with her only the simplest of cold picnics.

Once after two whole days of concentrated fishing the Queen Mother presented me with two salmon, one of which must have weighed about twenty pounds. "Do what you like with them," she said. "Why not give the staff a treat?"

As there was only one rather small and very old-fashioned refrigerator at Balmoral, I sent the large salmon to Clarence House to be put in the deep freeze to await a staff treat on my return, and cooked the smaller one according to the following recipe.

❀ *Balmoral Salmon*

1 *salmon*
1 *carrot*
1 *tablespoon vinegar*
10 *white peppercorns*
3 *or* 4 *slices onion*
parsley
3 *teaspoons salt*

Rinse salmon, drain and place in a large saucepan with the sliced carrot, onion, peppercorns, salt and vinegar. Cover with water and bring to the boil. Reduce heat and simmer until the flesh flakes easily. When dishing up, remove skin and bone without breaking the flesh and drain well. Cover with *Sauce au Citron*, garnish with parsley and serve with small boiled potatoes and cucumber salad.

The following recipes for crevettes (or shrimps) can be used either as a fish course in a dinner-party menu or as the main course of a light luncheon. In both recipes it is the pinch of cayenne pepper that gives the extra kick. Shrimps may be substituted for the Dublin Bay prawns. The shrimps or prawns are to be shelled, cleaned, and cooked in the simplest manner.

❀ *Prawns Piquant*

1 *pint Dublin Bay*
  prawns
1¼ *cups White Sauce*
½ *glass sherry or white*
  wine
2 *tablespoons tomato*
  sauce or 1½ *teaspoons*
  tomato purée
2 *tablespoons*
  mayonnaise
¾ *teaspoon salt*
pinch of cayenne
  pepper and pinch of
  sugar

To the white sauce add the sherry, tomato sauce, mayonnaise, salt, cayenne pepper and sugar. Blend well and simmer for two to three minutes. Pour over cooked prawns and garnish with parsley. Serves two.

❀ *Crevettes à la Reine*

1 *lb. shrimps*
3 *tablespoons butter*
3 *tablespoons flour*
1½ *cups fish stock*
pinch of cayenne
  pepper
1½ *teaspoons salt*
4 *tablespoons dry white*
  wine
4 *tablespoons cream*

Make the sauce by melting butter and then adding flour until absorbed. Pour in fish stock and seasoning and mix over a low heat. Add cream and stir until the mixture thickens. Stir in the wine and pour the sauce over cooked shrimps.
Serve in a pretty dish with Melba toast.

Here is a fish course, very simple ingredients, an easy method, but try it on your friends and like as not they will ask for the recipe. This is how we treat our fish in Sweden.

❁ *Cutlets of Plaice in Butter*

4 *fillets of plaice*
  (*or flounder*)
half a lemon
¼ *lb. butter*
2 *beaten eggs*
flour, salt, pepper

Skin, rinse and dry the fillets. Season with salt and pepper. Spread some flour on greaseproof paper. Place half the butter in a frying pan and place over a low heat. Heat gradually, but do not let the butter turn brown. Fold the fillets in half so that the inside is on the outside, turn them in the flour and dip in the beaten egg. Drop them in the hot butter and fry about three minutes on each side, until golden brown.

Dish up and garnish with lemon slices, fried parsley, and peas or spinach natural.

Turbot is a good rich fish and, served according to the following recipe as a main course, would need only a clear soup beforehand and perhaps a savoury afterwards to make a fine dinner party.

✿ *Turbot with Horseradish Sauce*

2 *lbs. turbot (or halibut) to four people*
2½ *cups boiling water*
8 *pimiento peppercorns*
2 *tablespoons flour*
3 *tablespoons butter*
1 *teaspoon salt*
1 *tablespoon grated horseradish*

Cut the turbot into cutlets about two inches thick without removing the bone. Place the cutlets in boiling water, add seasoning, cover with greaseproof paper and steam for ten to fifteen minutes. Strain the fish stock and thicken with the flour for a thick sauce, add more seasoning to taste, and simmer for five minutes. Remove from heat and whisk the cold butter in little by little. Keep hot. Carefully remove skin and bones from the fish and place the cutlets on a dish. Cover the fish with some of the sauce. Serve the rest separately, with the grated horseradish stirred in.

Serve with plain boiled potatoes in a white napkin.

I hope I am not alone in my admiration for the haddock. Haddock is a clean, nutritious fish with an individual nutty flavour, but I have a feeling it is regarded as the poor relation of the fish family.

The following recipes, once you have tried them, may do something to restore the status of this good fish.

I have served this next recipe throughout my cooking career, and out of all my fish dishes it is the one I cook most frequently in my own home.

✽ Grilled Haddock Special

2 *fillets of haddock*
2 *tablespoons butter*
½ *cup creamy milk*
4 *tomatoes*
1¼ *cups mashed potatoes*
salt, pepper and flour

Rinse and dry the haddock fillets thoroughly, cut each into two pieces and season with pepper and salt. Melt the butter and dip the fillets in the butter on both sides and then in the flour and again in the butter. Place them in a buttered fireproof dish ready for grilling. Baste once or twice under the grill. When fillets are coloured, pour the milk over them, remove from grill and place the dish containing the fish over a low heat on top of the stove to simmer for two or three minutes. Reduce the milky sauce a little so that the haddock is glazed. Meanwhile, skin and halve the tomatoes and remove the pips. Place them on a fireproof dish with a small knob of butter, season and pipe the mashed potatoes into the tomatoes. Heat in oven and serve with the fish.

The following recipe proves that haddock can behave itself in the grand manner at a smart dinner party.

❀ Crème de Haddock Fumé Tartare

1½ *lbs. smoked haddock*
¼ *lb. butter*
1 *cup fresh bread crumbs*
½ *cup milk*
4 *eggs*
salt and pepper
pinch of sugar

Remove the skin and bones of the haddock and put haddock through a mincer with the butter three times. Add the bread crumbs mixed with hot milk and allowed to cool. Mix well with the creamed fish. Whisk in the egg yolks, pepper, salt and sugar. Stir hard until the mixture resembles a smooth cream; then add the four egg whites beaten to a very stiff froth and blend in well. Fill a buttered basin or mould with the mixture and cover with greaseproof paper or foil. Steam for one hour on a low heat in boiling water, taking care not to let the water penetrate the fish cream, and keep the saucepan or *bain-marie* firmly covered.

When cooked, turn out on a dish and serve with a border of boiled rice garnished with shrimps or prawns.

Serve Tartare Sauce separately.

Picnics and Smorgasbord

THERE ARE two enormous advantages to eating out of doors: one physical, the other psychological. Firstly, eating in the open air relaxes the pressures under which most of us live and keens the appetite. Secondly, unwrapping the food from a well-appointed picnic hamper enhances the flavour and stimulates the imagination. Food, like women, benefits from a little mystery, which is why the contents of a picnic hamper should always be kept secret.

I have many ideas about picnics and none of them include sandwiches. It is true that sandwiches travel well, but so do hundreds of other foods that can be eaten out of doors. In fact, nowadays with the splendid selection of plastic containers there are few things that cannot travel.

The picnic food at Balmoral is transported in big old-fashioned hampers packed into the back of a shooting brake or Land Rover. Those capacious, laundry-basket type of hampers take a lot of beating. With good packing and a polythene top, even a fruit fool can arrive intact.

Careful preparation is the secret of a good picnic. What people want when they sit down in the great outdoors is *instant* food. Poultry and meat should be jointed or carved beforehand, for instance, so that the food can be unpacked and eaten right away.

I was accustomed to doing this anyway for the royal family, as they do not carve and all food is sent into the dining room ready for serving.

Here are just a few ideas which can be enlarged upon.

❀ Aspic Liver Pâté

2 lbs. calf's liver
1 lb. fatty bacon
6 eggs
1¼ cups light cream
4 tablespoons flour
3 or 4 sieved anchovies
2 tablespoons tomato
    sauce
2 tablespoons brandy
pepper, salt and a pinch
    of sugar
2½ cups aspic jelly
2 tablespoons sherry or
    white wine

Mince liver and three quarters of the bacon together and put it through a sieve or in a mixer. Mix the eggs, cream, flour and seasoning in a basin and add little by little to the liver mixture, stirring all the time. Add the sieved anchovies, the tomato sauce and the brandy. Bake in an oblong bread tin lined and covered with bacon and wrapped in foil in a medium oven for two hours. Allow the pâté to cool; then remove from tin and wash the tin. Add the wine to the aspic. Replace the pâté, cover with aspic jelly and allow to cool.

The following is more of a happy memory than a recipe, which is how good food should be thought of when it is related to a beautiful day, a perfect setting and happy people. It was consumed outside a disused Victorian palace belonging to the royal family near Loch N'Gair, and it was the sort of day on which you count your blessings.

❀ Royal Platter

a fillet (tenderloin) of
   beef
2 teaspoons gelatin
   dissolved in
   ½ cup beef stock
fresh lettuce
small braised onions
tomatoes
horseradish sauce

Roast the fillet of beef fifteen minutes to the pound in a hot oven, decreasing the heat slightly after the first half hour. Add a little gelatin stock to the natural juices when cooked, and as it cools spoon the juice over the beef so that it is glazed in jelly.

The beef was then sliced and rested on fresh lettuce leaves. With it I served small braised onions, slightly glazed, and skinned and pipped tomatoes filled with horseradish sauce mixed with cream.

This was accompanied by the following salad:

❁ Mixed Vegetable Salad

half a shredded white
    cabbage
2 grated carrots
half a cucumber cut in
    strips
1 chopped dessert apple
small pieces of leek cut
    in thin rings
1 tin petit pois
2 tablespoons chopped
    capers
2 or 3 oz. pickled
    cucumber and
    gherkins cut in rings

Mix ingredients together and moisten with salad dressing.

The salad dressing is my own version which I always keep by me winter and summer. It needs shaking up in a bottle before serving.

❁ McKee's Salad Dressing

1 tablespoon tarragon
    vinegar
3 tablespoons oil
½ teaspoon dry mustard
    dissolved in some
    vinegar
½ teaspoon pepper
½ teaspoon salt
pinch of sugar

Stir the ingredients together, then whisk a little.

Another cold joint highly convenient for picnics is:

❁ *Best End of Neck*

1 *best end of neck of lamb containing six cutlets**
1 *clove garlic*
2½ *cups aspic jelly*
tomatoes and mint jelly

Insert the garlic into the meat and roast the meat in a hot oven for a half hour in its own fat. Remove from pan and remove garlic. Chine and separate the cutlets with a sharp knife and remove unnecessary fat. Put together again and coat with aspic when cool. Serve with halved tomatoes filled with mint jelly.

With this I serve one of my favourite accompaniments:

❁ *Cucumber Salad*

1 *firm cucumber*
salt, pepper
1 *teaspoon sugar*
chopped mint
1 *tablespoon tarragon vinegar*

You can either peel the cucumbers or not, according to taste. Cut into thin slices and put in a basin. Season with pepper and salt, sugar and some mint. Let soak in a tablespoon (or more, according to the amount of cucumber) of tarragon vinegar.

* The U.S. equivalent would be a rack of lamb of six ribs or so.

On this same theme of meat cooled in its own juices with a rein-forced jelly and served with an interesting salad, there are many other variations.

Veal, for instance, cooled in a lightly spiced jelly and served with

❁ Cauliflower Salad

1 *large cauliflower*
1 *lemon*
nut oil
tarragon vinegar
seasoning
dry mustard
chopped chives or
   parsley

Cut the cauliflower into bouquets and boil in water with the juice of the lemon. Remove before the cauliflower becomes soft, drain in a napkin and while still hot put in a basin. Mix some McKee's Salad Dressing, pour onto the cauliflower and let it soak. Garnish with chives or parsley.

With cold ham:

❁ Fruit Salad

Squeeze the juice of one grapefruit and an orange. Slice some bananas, apples, grapes, orange and grapefruit and leave to soak overnight in the juice. Add some sugar to taste.

Take this dish on a picnic and watch it vanish:

❁ *Chicken Cream in Aspic*

4 lbs. stewing chicken
½ cup bread crumbs
a little warm milk
2½ cups cream
½ lb. bacon
1½ teaspoons sugar
seasoning
cucumber, olives, for
   decoration
1½ cups aspic jelly
   mixed with 2 table-
   spoons medium-sweet
   white wine

Cut away meat from chicken. Put three times through the mincer. Soften the bread crumbs with warm milk and mix together. Add pepper, salt and sugar and gradually add the cream, stirring all the time. Line a tin with half the bacon. Spread in the mixture and cover with the remaining bacon. Steam for an hour in water, either in the oven or on top of the stove, taking care that it does not boil over. Turn out when cool, clean the tin, decorate the bottom with cut olives and cucumber, replace the chicken cream and pour over the aspic jelly. Cool and turn out onto a bed of lettuce.

Can be made with veal instead of chicken.

A nice complement to this dish is a salad with the following sauce:

❁ *Salad Sauce with Eggs*

½ *teaspoon dry mustard*
2 *tablespoons vinegar*
pepper, salt and pinch
of sugar
4 *hard-boiled eggs*
2 *raw egg yolks*
½ *cup cream*
lettuce and chives

Mix the mustard with the vinegar, pepper, salt and sugar to a smooth paste. Sieve the hard-boiled egg yolks into a small basin and blend in raw egg yolks and half the cream. Add the vinaigrette sauce gradually, stirring all the time, and finish with the rest of the cream.

Pour over a salad of lettuce and chopped chives and sprinkle with the chopped whites of eggs.

The nice thing about Scandinavian smorgasbord is that it is so versatile. For a buffet supper you can serve fairly substantial dishes such as small *frikadeller,* minced beefsteaks, sautéed kidneys, mushrooms, slices of beef and so on. As cocktail canapés, small open-face sandwiches on interesting bread make a contrast both of flavour and of appearance. For example, on a piece of brown bread I might sieve the yolk of a hard-boiled egg, placing it in the middle of the bread, surround the yolk with chopped white of egg and garnish with an anchovy. This is rather a simple example, but it illustrates the contrast. There are no exact rules or recipes. It is a matter of inspiration and piquant ingredients, bearing in mind the central theme of contrast.

First some ingredients. If I were preparing a table of smorgasbord I should start with the following ingredients:

Thinly sliced ham; cooked salmon; crabmeat; smoked eel; herrings in marinade; liver pâté; *shrimps; sardines; anchovies;*

85

mussels; hard-boiled eggs; asparagus in vinaigrette sauce; small new beetroots in sweetened tarragon vinegar; fruit salad; cucumber salad; celery; radishes; spring onions; tinned red and yellow pimientos; water cress; lettuce, parsley and chopped chives for decoration; and plenty of homemade mayonnaise.

To start you off:

Cut brown, white and rye bread into circles, squares or triangles. It should not be too thin if it is to support some of the moisture or more substantial garnishes—but not doorsteps, of course.

Fold ham slices into cornets and fill either with a little fruit salad and mayonnaise or with mayonnaise and asparagus tips; place on a lettuce leaf on white buttered bread.

Mix some crabmeat, chopped hard-boiled eggs and mayonnaise together. Place on dark-brown bread and decorate with mayonnaise and chopped chives. The same can be done with a salmon mixture spread on bread and decorated with cucumber slices. For a professional look the mayonnaise can be piped.

The appearance of the smorgasbord table is important, too. One thing we always have in Sweden is a large cucumber with the middle scooped out like a canoe and filled with Russian salad. Celery sticks filled with Danish blue cheese also look decorative and are delicious to eat.

At hot smorgasbord parties, the guests walk around the table with little plates and forks helping themselves. I have only to think of a smorgasbord party to wish I were actually giving one. Now at this minute I would offer: calves' kidneys sautéed in port wine; anchovies rolled in bread crumbs and deep-fried; little omelettes stuffed with white sauce and asparagus tips or creamed sweetbreads; small onions filled with chopped-up meat, braised in brown butter sauce and glazed in sugared aspic.

Another occasion might produce a completely different smorgasbord table. In fact, no two parties are ever alike.

One thing that never alters, however, is the traditional hot cup always offered at Christmas parties in Sweden—*julglögg*. I cannot think of it without seeing the big red Christmas candles, and drawn curtains in a gaily decorated room.

Many people in Britain regard wine cups and the like with distrust. They prefer their drinks straight. They have good reason. Most of us have suffered at one time or another from the indiscriminate cup where everything is mixed together with dire results. The other familiar offering is a sickly lemonade-type substitute that gets nobody anywhere!

The following prescription for Swedish *glögg* is especially suitable for consumption on the premises of draughty English country houses on a cold winter's day. In Sweden we always drink it on Christmas morning. In England I can imagine it going down particularly well as a stirrup cup on Boxing Day, or at almost any time during a freeze-up. For a Swedish-style party, serve it with smorgasbord.

❀ *Julglögg*

½ *bottle of vodka*
½ *bottle of port wine*
10 *cardamom seeds*
1 *oz. muscat raisins*
1 *small cinnamon stick*
4 *cloves*
1 *oz. blanched and skinned sweet almonds*
2 *lumps sugar or 2 tablespoons brown sugar*

Pour the wine and vodka into a silver chafing dish or stainless-steel saucepan and warm until hot. Rinse the raisins in hot water and add to the *glögg* together with the rest of the ingredients. Cover and heat. Just before the drink is ready to serve, set fire to it with a match, burn quickly and extinguish with the lid.

Serve and drink as hot as possible. *Skål!*

Lunch and Dinner Menus

It can't be wrong to want to please people with your cooking. And one asks for nothing in return except that people should enjoy themselves. The general mood of health, happiness and benevolence bestowed by a good meal is ample thanks to the cook.

I once worked in a castle in Sweden where they toasted the cook in champagne between every course. A charming idea, but frankly the cooking suffered in the end.

Nowadays most intelligent women are wonderful cooks. But many from time to time feel the need to provide something rather impressive for a special occasion. Perhaps they have to entertain their husbands' business friends, or in-laws, or some rather grand acquaintances, or maybe just someone they love.

Sometimes it is necessary to pull out all the stops and do better than your best. How do you define the thin line between good cooking and making a good impression? I don't like showy cooking myself, but I can't pretend that I have never been influenced by the circumstances of a special occasion.

People often ask me if I was made nervous by the illustrious names on the guest list when I was cooking at Clarence House. Well, I would have been, of course, if I had known who was to be there beforehand. But often the Comptroller's guest list, issued a fortnight in advance, simply stated the number of guests to a particular meal. I was fortified by that, and told myself they were just people. Once there were four queens to lunch. Luckily I didn't know until afterward when I received a message that the royal ladies had thoroughly enjoyed my *sole véronique*. Had I known I might have been influenced to try something grander. Yet *sole véronique* at its best is certainly a dish to set before a queen.

Another time, when the Queen Mother and Princess Margaret gave a joint party attended by the Queen and Prince Philip, the guest list went like this: the Duchess of Kent, Mr. Billy Wallace, the Duke and Duchess of Norfolk, Mr. Noel Coward, the Master of Elphinstone, Mr. Peter Cazalet, Lord Salisbury, Mr. Peter Ustinov, the Hon. Mrs. Wills and Mr. Norman Hackforth. How to please such a cosmopolitan party?

The fact is that on special occasions most women feel the need to provide something special. It makes them less anxious, somehow. So it was with royalty. I would make a list of initial suggestions, and the Queen or Queen Mother would select the final dishes very carefully.

We had some very simple menus at Clarence House, but also some very grand ones. I enjoyed doing both.

The following are a mixture of both. Some simple, some complicated. I will warn you about the complicated ones. However, if you are looking for a contract, prestige, a man or just a challenge, you will not be deterred.

Oeufs en Cocotte aux Tomates
Chicken Américaine
Bouchées aux Champignons
Beans and Crisp Potatoes
Salad
Banana Caramel

This is a fairly simple lunch for four people. Not obviously grand, but delights with small surprises.

🏵 *Oeufs en Cocotte aux Tomates*

4 *eggs*
2 *tomatoes*
½ *cup heavy cream*
½ *cup grated Parmesan cheese*
seasoning

Skin the tomatoes. A quick way of doing this is to hold them over a low flame on a fork. Grease china cocotte dishes with butter and add slices of seasoned tomatoes. Slide a whole raw egg into each dish. Cover each egg with a spoonful of cream and sprinkle some grated cheese on top. Put under the grill to brown. When golden brown, place in a moderate oven for five minutes so that the eggs are almost set but still wobbly.

🏵 *Chicken Américaine*

2 *broilers, quartered*
2 *beaten eggs*
seasoning
garlic salt
bread crumbs
½ *lb. butter*
flour

Remove the skin of the chickens, then bone them by cutting down the middle of each joint. Season with pepper, salt and a little garlic salt. Flour, egg and bread-crumb the chicken pieces and fry gently in butter until golden brown. Place on a buttered tin and put in a moderate oven for fifteen minutes to finish.

❀ Bouchées aux Champignons

4 puff-pastry shells
  (from the baker)
½ lb. mushrooms
2½ cups milk
1 tablespoon flour
knob of butter
pinch of sugar
pepper and salt

Slice the mushrooms, pour one and a half cups of milk over them in a saucepan, bring to the boil, season and simmer for two to three minutes. Dilute the flour with half a cup of milk, add to the mushrooms and cook slowly for ten minutes. Remove from the heat and add the butter and sugar. Fill the shells with this mixture.

Serve the chicken in a dish with the mushroom *bouchées*, beans (fresh or frozen), some thinly cut fried potatoes, and salad according to season.

❀ Banana Caramel

4 bananas
¼ lb. butter
4 tablespoons cream
1½ teaspoons orange
  curaçao or ¾ teaspoon
  vanilla essence
4 tablespoons corn
  syrup

Mash the bananas and fry in butter. Remove, cool, and add the orange curaçao or vanilla and the cream. Fill some wide-topped glasses with this mixture.

To make the caramel topping: Heat the corn syrup in a saucepan and boil until brown. Pour into a buttered tin and spread thinly. When cold, chip and sprinkle onto the banana mixture.

The following is the menu to produce only when there is a lot at stake, because, frankly, it will take you about all day. It is not that any of the courses are particularly complicated, but there is quite a lot of detail in the preparation, and, as all the dishes are rather subtle in flavour, any skimping or hurrying will render them pointless. I cannot remember the particular occasion on which I produced this menu at Clarence House, but I do recall that the Queen, like most people, was a little doubtful about the venison. All that I can say about this recipe for venison is that it is different and that I received a personal thank-you and further requests for it.

In preparing this menu I would be inclined to make the consommé the day before. Then get the ice cream off first, then the venison, leaving the final cooking of the turbot until last. The recipes serve eight.

Consommé Julienne
Turbot Fritters, Tartare Sauce
Braised Venison
Boiled Potatoes, Peas and Beans
Crème aux Marrons

❀ *Consommé Julienne*

1 *lb. shin of beef*
1 *lb. shin of veal*
1 *carrot*
1 *onion*
1 *celery stalk*
10 *white peppercorns*
2½ *quarts cold water*
1½ *teaspoons sugar*
1 *tablespoon salt*
1 *clove*
*carrot, parsnip and
    parsley for garnish*

Cut the meat into small pieces and put into the water. Heat slowly, gradually bringing to the boil. Remove scum and add the vegetables to the meat. Add the salt, peppercorns, sugar and clove and simmer over a low heat for three hours or more. Boil the carrot and parsnip garnish for a couple of minutes and cut into thin strips. Strain the soup and let it cool. Skim off fat when cold. Strain through muslin, save two tablespoons of the meat, cut into small pieces and put back into the soup. Garnish with the thinly cut vegetables and serve very hot with cheese straws or croutons.

❀ *Turbot Fritters*

2 *lbs. filleted turbot (or
    halibut)*
salt and pepper
lemon
2 *eggs*
1 *cup sifted all-purpose
    flour*
¾ *cup milk*
2 *tablespoons oil*

Wash the fish and dry thoroughly. Cut up into fingers, season with pepper and salt and a squeeze of lemon. Sprinkle with flour.

To make the batter: Beat the milk into the flour, beat in the eggs, then the oil. Continue beating until smooth.

Dip the fingers into the batter and fry in deep oil until golden brown. Serve with Tartare Sauce.

93

✿ *Braised Venison*

4 lbs. fillet of venison
¾ lb. fat larding bacon
4 tablespoons red
currant jelly
1 wineglass of rather
vinegary burgundy
½ cup cream
2 tablespoons butter
4 tablespoons flour
1 carrot
1 onion
2½ cups stock or water
pepper, salt, garlic salt

Wrap the larding bacon round the fillet of venison. Melt the butter in a saucepan and brown the meat. Cut up the carrot and onion and put in the pan with the stock or water. Add the pepper, salt and garlic salt and braise in a low oven for two hours. Remove the meat and vegetables from the pan and skim off the fat. Mix the flour with some water and stir into the gravy. Let it boil on top of the stove for a few minutes to reduce the gravy. Strain into another saucepan and add the red currant jelly and more stock if necessary. Add the wine and simmer for three minutes. Remove from heat and stir in the cream. Dish up the venison and spoon a little of the sauce over it. Serve the rest of the sauce separately.

Only the plainest of vegetables, such as small boiled potatoes, peas or beans are necessary with this dish.

❁ Crème aux Marrons

2½ cups heavy cream
1 lb. chestnuts
½ cup sugar
4 tablespoons cold
* butter*
a couple of drops of
* vanilla essence or*
* maraschino to taste*
1 orange

Peel the chestnuts and boil in a cup of water until tender. Drain. Put the chestnuts through a metal sieve, add the butter and sugar and mix to a smooth cream. Put the mixture into a forcing bag and pipe round and round the border of a silver dish. Whip the cream and add the vanilla essence or maraschino; sweeten if necessary. Pile into the centre of the dish and decorate with pipped, peeled and sweetened orange slices.

This is a luncheon menu which, if I may say so, is *discreetly* good and well balanced. There are several rather distinctive touches which will show imagination but not flamboyance. A splendid menu for in-laws or deals.

Grilled Ugly Fruit
Tournedos Sautés
Pommes Frites, Petit Pois, Salade
Pineapple Cake

❁ Grilled Ugly Fruit

half an ugly fruit to
* each person*
sugar

Cut and pip the ugly fruit like a grapefruit. Cover with sugar and grill until brown. Serve hot.

❀ *Tournedos Sautés*

1 *tournedos steak (or filet mignon) to each person*
butter for frying
2 *tablespoons butter*
1½ *teaspoons flour*
1¼ *cups stock*
½ *lb. beef or veal kidney*
2 *tablespoons Madeira wine*

Fry steaks in butter for five minutes on each side. Remove from pan and keep hot though not cooking. Melt butter in a saucepan, work in the flour until brown, stir in the stock and the chopped kidney. Cook for fifteen minutes and add the Madeira. Serve the tournedos with the sauce poured over them.

Nothing better with it than French-fried potatoes, peas and green salad.

❀ *Pineapple Cake*

1 *fresh pineapple*
1 *cup butter*
1 *cup sugar*
3 *eggs*
1½ *cups sifted all-purpose flour*
1½ *heaped teaspoons baking powder*
6 *tablespoons cornstarch*

Pulp the pineapple by grating or putting into a mixer, and add sugar to taste. Put in a greased fireproof dish and keep warm. Cream the butter and sugar together and add the other ingredients. Put the cake mixture on top of the pineapple pulp and bake in a moderate oven for three quarters of an hour. Loosen carefully. Turn out and serve with cream.

Here is a menu for which I have a particular affection. Nearly all the ingredients are good, unpretentious and valuable. In that way it is a simple menu. But success depends on a certain amount of planning ahead. The pudding can be done ahead, but the soup should be served straight away. If you are cook-hostess, the veal will keep while the other courses are being served, but ideally the fish should be served at the last minute.

This dinner party is for six.

Cocky-leeky Soup
Sole à la Sauce Rémoulade
Veal Cutlets Farcis
Cucumber Salad and Small Boiled Potatoes
Orange Fromage

❀ Cocky-leeky Soup

5 *cups veal bone stock*
2 *large potatoes*
2 *leeks*
seasoning
pinch of sugar
2 *eggs*
½ *cup cream*
½ *cup grated Gruyère cheese*
knob of butter

Peel and cube the potatoes; skin the leeks and cut the white part into rings. Put the vegetables into the stock and cook until soft; add seasoning and sugar. Whip the eggs and cream in a bowl. Take the vegetables out of the stock, remove from heat and thicken with the beaten eggs and cream. Add the butter and, last thing, the cheese. Keep hot, but do not allow to cook as otherwise the soup will curdle.

The making of this soup merits your closest attention.

97

❀ *Sole à la Sauce Rémoulade*

2 *filleted Dover soles*
1¼ *cups fish stock*
2 *cups mashed potatoes*
seasoning
Sauce Rémoulade
1¼ *cups cooked shrimps*
parsley

Rinse fillets and dry well. Season and place in a tin with the stock. Cover with greaseproof paper and poach in a moderate oven for fifteen minutes. Border a nice dish with the mashed potatoes, drain the fish and arrange in the middle. Coat with the *Sauce Rémoulade* and decorate with shrimps and parsley.

❀ *Veal Cutlets Farcis*

2 *lbs. veal from the leg*
½ *cup fresh bread crumbs*
2 *eggs*
½ *cup warm milk*
¾ *teaspoon sugar*
pepper, salt, pinch of nutmeg
½ *cup white wine*
butter

Cut the meat from the leg. (Use the bone to make stock.) Put the meat twice through the mincer on a medium plate. Mix the bread crumbs with the milk and work it into the mince. Add the beaten eggs, seasoning, sugar and nutmeg. Mix well and mould into cutlets. Fry in butter on both sides for ten minutes. Remove from the pan and keep warm. Add some more butter to the frying pan if necessary and pour in some stock and the wine; simmer fast to reduce the quantity and pour some onto the cutlets. Serve the rest separately.

Dish up on a platter bordered with plain boiled rice and, heaped in the centre, button mushrooms sautéed in butter. Instead of a cooked vegetable, try cucumber salad.

❀ *Orange Fromage*

6 *small juicy oranges*
6 *tablespoons sugar*
2½ *cups orange jelly*
½ *lb. cream cheese*
roasted flaked almonds
2½ *cups water*

Decapitate the oranges and remove pips and fibrous centre, but otherwise leave whole. Put the oranges in a saucepan of water, add the sugar and cook gently until soft. Cool in the syrup. Either make a jelly with the syrup and unflavoured gelatin or use packaged orange gelatin. Place the oranges in a dish and pour in the jelly just before setting point. Pipe the cream cheese into the oranges and spoon over some of the jelly to make a glaze. Decorate with the almonds. Serve very cold.

Dinner at eight . . . and you could set your clock by the Queen's appearance at the dinner table with her guests. This punctuality, I am sure, is dictated by a natural consideration for the people who work for her. Dinner at eight meant that on a good day I could be finished in the kitchen by 10 P.M. I always saw the dinner through down to the serving of the coffee, although of course I did not have to wash up. After this I went to my room and wrote out the menus for the following day. Oddly enough, that was my greatest headache. The menus had to be in French, and, being no scholar of languages, I used to struggle for hours with the language of haute cuisine. Eventually I found a wonderful but very expensive book which contained all the terms I needed, though I was still conscious of the odd mistake. However, the Queen, who speaks excellent French, was very kind about this and tactfully ignored any errors.

When you are cooking for royalty, of course, every day is in a sense a special occasion. Two very special guests at Clarence House before Princess Elizabeth became Queen were her mother and father. On the occasions of their visits, the menu was a matter of detailed selection.

The following is a right royal menu, in that all the ingredients are of the very best. The preparation is a matter of love, care and patience, and in all fairness I will say that I have never attempted this menu as a cook-hostess. If you are to cook and to appear at your own dinner table, you will need help. The soup, pudding and *foie gras* can be prepared in advance, but the fish and chicken courses must have close attention at dinnertime.

Consommé à la Charlotte
Turbot à la Crème Citron
Filets de Volaille à la Princesse
Pointes d'Asperges
Sauce aux Champignons
Salade Française
Parfait Ananas Royale
Petits Fours
Foie Gras Chantilly Strasbourg
Macédoine de Fruits

❀ *Consommé à la Charlotte*

1 *lb. of shin beef*
1 *lb. of shin of veal*
5 *pints water*
1 *carrot*
1 *onion*
1 *stick of celery*
10 *whole white*
 peppercorns
1 *clove*
1½ *teaspoons salt*
1½ *teaspoons sugar*
1 *glass medium-sweet*
 white wine
1 *lb. whole roasted*
 walnuts
½ *lb. muscat grapes*

Make a clear consommé according to the method given for Consommé Julienne and remove all the vegetables. Allow to cool, skim off fat and strain through a muslin cloth. Then add the wine and serve very hot, with the scraped walnuts and the pipped and skinned grapes floated in each dish. This soup improves if kept overnight at the cooling stage.

I had the nerve to call this consommé "Charlotte" after one of my own names, as this soup is very much my own creation.

❀ *Turbot à la Crème Citron*

4 *fillets of turbot (or*
 halibut)
1 *glass white wine*
1 *glass fish stock*
1 *lemon*
parsley

Poach the fillets in the wine and the stock in a moderate oven for fifteen minutes. Remove the fish from the juice. Dish up and cover with *Sauce au Citron*. Decorate with parsley and thinly sliced lemon.

❀ *Filets de Volaille à la Princesse*

2 *breasts of chicken*
¼ *lb. veal*
¼ *lb. ham*
⅓ *cup cream*
butter for cooking
2 *oranges and water*
  cress for decoration
seasoning

Make a forcemeat by mincing the veal and ham together and mixing with the cream. Season. Halve the breasts of chicken, divide the forcemeat, put equal portions on the inside of the pieces of chicken and fry gently in butter until golden brown. Then place in a medium oven and bake for ten minutes.

Dish up the chicken fillets and glaze them with some of their own juice. Plunge the oranges into boiling water, quarter, remove pips but leave the skins. Decorate the chicken fillets with the orange quarters and water cress.

❀ *Sauce aux Champignons*

½ *lb. mushrooms*
1 *cup light cream*
1 *cup chicken stock*
1 *tablespoon flour*
seasoning
¾ *teaspoon sugar*
2 *tablespoons butter*

Slice the mushrooms and boil them for two minutes in the cream. Make a sauce from the chicken stock thickened with flour. Add the mushrooms, seasoning and sugar and, lastly, the cold butter.

Serve the *Sauce aux Champignons* and asparagus tips separately.

❁ Salade Française

*Fresh lettuce hearts in
French dressing*

❁ Parfait Ananas Royale

1 *pint vanilla ice cream*
1 *pineapple or a large
tin of pineapple rings*
¾ *cup sugar*

Roughly grate half the pineapple and add to the ice cream. Put the mixture in a tin or mould and freeze for three hours. Make some caramel by placing the sugar in a heavy saucepan over a gentle heat and dissolving slowly without stirring. Boil steadily to a rich brown and pour into a greased tin. Allow to cool; then crush. Turn the parfait out onto a silver or crystal dish and decorate with thinly sliced pineapple rings. Sprinkle the crushed caramel artistically.
Serve with *petits fours*.

❁ *Foie Gras Chantilly Strasbourg*

½ lb. pâté de foie gras
½ cup whipped cream
1¼ cups aspic jelly (set)
lettuce
fresh fruit salad made
  from slices of peeled
  and pipped grapefruit,
  pear, apple and peach
  soaked in grapefruit
  juice to preserve the
  colour

Sieve the *foie gras* and mix it with the whipped cream. Have ready two tablespoons in hot water and scoop the *foie gras* into a silver dish. This will give the impression of eggs in a basket. Sprinkle the chopped aspic round the *foie gras* and pile the fruit on lettuce leaves in the same dish. Serve with Melba toast.

And the best of British luck!

As I LOOK back upon my view of the Princess at Clarence House, I realize it was of course purely a domestic one. I saw her at home, happy, relaxed and smiling. In fact, up to the time of her first Trooping of the Colours in the Horse Guards' Parade Ground, I had never actually seen Princess Elizabeth in her official capacity.

There was a sort of foreboding about this occasion when Princess Elizabeth deputised for her father, the King, who was too ill to take his part in the ceremony, which has to be performed by the monarch on horseback.

I was standing at the bottom of the stairs at Clarence House when the Princess came down dressed in her uniform. As always on official occasions, she was unhurried, with time in hand for a few words with whoever happened to be about.

Turning to me, she indicated her hat and said, "My father designed this. Do you like it?"

All at once she looked different: the unfamiliar uniform, the tricorne hat and the grave, composed expression.

"Now," she said with a slight smile, "you see how I look on duty."

Somehow it was a heartbreaking moment. Later I watched her as she came down the Mall on horseback, so small, so serious. And for the first time, but not the last, my heart turned over at her loneliness.

Everyone will remember how Princess Elizabeth flew from London Airport on the royal tour of Kenya in 1952 only to return a few days later as Queen of England.

As soon as the Queen arrived home we were immediately plunged into hectic activity. Clarence House was permanently overflowing with ministers and officials, and in the rush and confusion there was no time to think of anything except feeding them.

It was perfectly clear to us that the Queen was under a very great strain at that time. The closeness between herself and her father was well known, and I think she dreaded the move from Clarence House to the palace, where there were so many sad associations. Every time the subject of a changeover was broached we were told that the Queen wished to remain at Clarence House as long as possible.

Soon, however, with more officials crowding into the place and more affairs of State to attend to every day, it became clear that the Queen could no longer operate from Clarence House.

Sometime after the King's funeral, I offered the Queen my sincere and humble condolences on her father's death.

Her reply, so simple and moving, will stay with me all my life.

"Yes," she said slowly, "he was a good man."

A good man. From the Queen of England there is no higher praise.

Before the Queen left to move into the Belgian Suite at Buckingham Palace, she said goodbye to all the staff who were not accompanying her; and I received a white-and-gold enamel brooch with her initials.

Everybody at that time was under six months' official notice, and the new appointments would take months to sort out. There was certainly no place for a woman cook in the all-male stronghold of Buckingham Palace. Meanwhile I had been asked to go to Royal Lodge, Windsor, which actually belonged to the Queen Mother. The Queen and her family used to weekend there as guests.

Before she left, the Queen told me that she was glad she would still be able to enjoy my cooking at weekends. "I am sure you will like it at Royal Lodge," she said, and asked me if there was anything I was worried about.

I told her that I was happy to go to Royal Lodge but didn't know what to do with Poppet, my Siamese cat.

The Queen smiled. "Take him to Royal Lodge," she said. "There couldn't be a better place for a cat."

So off we went—the Queen to her palace, and Poppet and myself to Windsor, where we were indeed very happy.

Now, at sixty-six, I spend a good deal of my time in the garden—a return to that most fulfilling of hobbies which I first learned to enjoy all those years ago in Sweden.

But even now I get offers to cook for well-known people who like my sort of food, and off I go for a few days or weeks. And I still find the challenge of providing good food for people who appreciate it an irresistible stimulus.

I started cooking because I liked it and found it was a way in which I could please people and add to their well-being. I have tried never to lose sight of this simple theme, and all the nice, exciting things that have happened to me in my life have sprung from this philosophy. If I had followed a different course, I could have been richer, but not, I believe, so happy.

One more thing I should like to point out. All the best things that happened to me occurred late in life. I married late, I reached the peak of my career when I was over fifty. Even now I have discovered a new and useful phase in my life. I do not believe that there is ever a time in a woman's life when she need feel bored or useless.

And the root of all this happiness? The humble art of cooking.

Index

109